# FEDERAL LAW OF EMPLOYMENT DISCRIMINATION

## IN A NUTSHELL

### THIRD EDITION

By

## MACK A. PLAYER
Associate Dean and Professor of Law
Florida State University
College of Law

ST. PAUL, MINN.
WEST PUBLISHING CO.
1992

COPYRIGHT © 1976, 1981 WEST PUBLISHING CO.
COPYRIGHT © 1992 By WEST PUBLISHING CO.
                            610 Opperman Drive
                            P.O. Box 64526
                            St. Paul, MN 55164–0526
All rights reserved
Printed in the United States of America

**Library of Congress Cataloging-in-Publication Data**

Player, Mack A.
    Federal law of employment discrimination in a nutshell / Mack A.
  Player. — 3rd ed.
      p.    cm. — (Nutshell series)
    Includes index.
    ISBN 0–314–00128–X
    1. Discrimination in employment—Law and legislation—United
  States.  I. Title.  II. Series.
  KF3464.Z9P55   1992
  344.73'01133—dc20
  [347.3041133]                                              91–38108
                                                                 CIP

**ISBN** 0–314–00128–X

 TEXT IS PRINTED ON 10% POST CONSUMER RECYCLED PAPER         PRINTED WITH SOY INK

Player, Empl.Discrim.NS 3rd
2nd Reprint—1994

To
Guy Allen Player
My Father

\*

# PREFACE

The focus of this work is discrimination in the work place based on race, sex, national origin, religion, age, and disability. Other aspects of work-place discrimination, such as free speech of public employees and discrimination based on economic activity, are touched on herein but are more appropriately and more fully treated elsewhere. See West Nutshells by Professor Leslie on labor law, Professors Barron and Dienes on constitutional law, Professor Vieira on constitutional civil rights, and Professors Hood, Hardy & Lewis on workers' compensation and employee protection laws.

The emphasis of this work is on federal law. State legislation often parallels and occasionally goes beyond the protections of federal law, such as by prohibiting discrimination based on sexual preferences or marital status. Aside from the summary of the common law background, state law is noted at most in passing.

Needless to say the treatment herein is summary. A more thorough analysis is available in the hornbook by the author, Player, Employment Discrimination Law (West, 1988). Different perspectives which thoroughly analyze this area of

law are Sullivan, Zimmer, Richards, Employment
Discrimination Law (2d Ed. 1988) and Shulman &
Abernathy, The Law of Equal Employment Oppor-
tunity (1989). A regularly cited casebook with
commentaries is Schlei & Grossman, Employment
Discrimination Law.

Case citations in the text refer only to the
court and date. A full citation is found in the
table of cases. Citations do not include irrelevant
subsequent histories such as certiorari denied.

I have used the descriptive, non-scientific
terms "black" and "white" to refer to the respective Negroid and Caucasian races. Notwithstanding increasing popular use of "African–American"
as a substitute for "black," that term, on one hand,
is more narrow than race, suggesting a particular
combination of citizenship and geographical origins. On the other hand, Americans of "white"
and Asian races with family origins in Africa may
consider themselves "African–Americans." To
avoid confusion, the term "African–American" was
avoided.

After the book was in page proofs the President signed the Civil Rights Act of 1991. At this
stage I was able to insert into the text references to
key provisions of this important Act, but as these
text revisions had to meet the production requirements of a book in its final pre-publication stage
these new inserts occasionally are not ideally complete. To meet this shortcoming I added an appen-

dix which contains in full the relevant portions of the Civil Rights Act of 1991 and a short explanation drawn from the Act's legislative history.

I must thank Florida State University College of Law for providing me with a research leave to work on this nutshell. My invaluable co-participant in initially writing and ultimately editing this work was Jeanne M.L. Player. In addition, Linda Griffiths, J.D. Florida State 1990, read the manuscript and offered many helpful substantive and editorial comments.

M.A.P.

December, 1991

\*

# OUTLINE

## PART I.  BACKGROUND AND OVERVIEW

## PART II. THE CORE OF EMPLOYMENT DISCRIMINATION LAW: THE BASIS OF LIABILITY

# PART III. PROTECTED CLASSES AND APPLICATION OF BASIC CONCEPTS

## PART V. ENVIRONMENTAL DISCRIMINATION AND WORK PLACE RULES

## PART VII. ENFORCEMENT PROCEDURES

# TABLE OF CASES

**References are to Pages**

## TABLE OF CASES

# TABLE OF CASES

## TABLE OF CASES

## TABLE OF CASES

## TABLE OF CASES

# TABLE OF CASES

## TABLE OF CASES

XL

## TABLE OF CASES

# FEDERAL LAW OF EMPLOYMENT DISCRIMINATION

## IN A NUTSHELL

### Third Edition

\*

# PART I

# BACKGROUND AND OVERVIEW

## CHAPTER 1

## THE COMMON LAW

### § 1.01  The Traditional "Employment At Will" Rule

Since the late 19th century the common law in the United States defined employment as an "at will" relationship.  Employers were free to hire or reject any applicant at whim, to establish inequitable work-place rules, to set arbitrary levels of compensation, and to terminate the relationship without notice and for any reason or no reason. *Pearson v. Youngstown Sheet & Tube Co.* (7th Cir. 1964).  Free from legal interference, employers could refuse to hire racial minorities, segregate the work-force, assign unpleasant work to women and racial minorities, and deny to them opportunities for advancement.  They could pay discriminatory wage rates for equal work and arbitrarily demand differing levels of job performance.

Similarly, labor unions were not subject to significant legal restraint.  The only protection was the

1

contract formed between the individual member and the organization. The constitution or by-laws of the union constituted an offer which was accepted by the individual upon becoming a member. If these charter documents permitted expulsion only upon "good cause," the courts might enforce this contract. *NLRB v. Allis–Chalmers Mfg. Co.* (S.Ct. 1967). This provided little protection against arbitrary treatment of members, however, and no protection for individuals discriminatorily denied admission. See *Steele v. Louisville & Nashville R. Co.* (S.Ct.1944).

## § 1.02　Modern Evolution: Exceptions to the "At Will" Rule

### a. *Implied Obligation of Good Faith and Fair Dealing*

Modern contract theory provides that "[e]very contract imposes upon each party a duty of good faith and fair dealing in its performance and its enforcement." § 205, Rest.Cont.2d. The implied duty of good faith and fair dealing prohibits the exercise of a power of termination except for reasons which are honest in fact, consistent with accepted norms of reasonableness, and germane to the contractual expectations of the parties. It violates the duty of good faith and fair dealing for an employer to fire an employee because she refused to have a sexual relationship, *Monge v. Beebe Rubber Co.* (N.H.1974), or to discharge a long term employee to avoid pension obligations.  *Fortune v. National Cash Register Co.* (Mass.1977).

The vast majority of courts, however, have held that employment contracts do not contain an implied covenant of good faith and fair dealing, either because the "at will" doctrine is so much a part of the common law that any alteration must be legislative, *Murphy v. American Home Products Corp.* (N.Y.1983), or because they believe that any remedy for abusive discharge must come from a finding that the discharge undermines public policy. *Brockmeyer v. Dun & Bradstreet* (Wis.1983).

### b.  The Tort of Wrongful Discharge: Undermining Public Policy

By 1960, state courts began to recognize that an employer which discharged an employee for refusing to violate the law was using economic power to force illegal activity.  Consequently, to discharge a worker for refusing to commit perjury was "wrongful."  *Petermann v. International Broth. of Teamsters, Local 396* (Cal.App.1959). Similarly, punishing an employee for exercising a right under legislation designed to protect the worker (e.g., workers' compensation or occupational safety) "wrongfully" undermines the public policies advanced by the social legislation.  Thus, a majority of the states today hold that it is wrongful to discharge a worker for refusing to perform an illegal act or to retaliate against a worker for asserting a personal statutory right.  *Frampton v.*

*Central Indiana Gas Co.* (Ind.1973). Some courts recognize that enforcement of the law requires communication between persons with access to key information and government enforcement agencies. Because it undermines the enforcement of the laws, the discharge of a "whistleblower" is "wrongful." *Harless v. First Nat. Bank* (W.Va. 1978).

A few courts continue to refuse to make any exception to the "at will" doctrine, and those that recognize a "public policy" exception require the discharged employee to identify a specific, defined, and fundamental policy undermined by the discharge. *Brockmeyer v. Dun & Bradstreet* (Wis. 1983). The quality of the employer's product, the employer's accounting methods, or the general ethics of the employer's actions do not trigger policies so defined or fundamental that firing an employee for complaining about them is wrongful. *Adler v. American Standard Corp.* (Md.1981).

If the discharge is considered "wrongful," most courts classify the employer's action as tortious and award damages for lost wages and consequential injuries naturally flowing from the employer's wrongful conduct, such as pain, suffering, and loss of reputation. Punitive damages are a remedy for malicious attempts to punish the employee who attempted to advance the public policy. Cf. *Foley v. Interactive Data Corp.* (Cal.1988) (tort-like compensatory and punitive damages *not* available).

The "public policy" exception to the "at will" relationship has not been extended to hiring or job assignment. Unless restrained by statute, employers remain free to refuse to enter the employment relationship for any reason. *Hurley v. Allied Chemical Corp.* (W.Va.1980).

## § 1.03  Expressed Individual Contracts

Occasionally, employers and individual employees execute written contracts that specify the conditions under which termination of the contract is authorized (e.g., "just cause"), and provide procedures for resolution of whether conditions for termination have been satisfied (e.g., "personal interview by the personnel director"). Such contracts are enforced. In many cases terms are stated informally, such as through an exchange of letters or in a manual or handbook outlining job tenure and discipline procedures. Traditionally, such informal statements were not deemed contractual, but today if the employee reasonably considered the statements as promissory commitments, they are enforced. *Wooley v. Hoffmann–La Roche, Inc.* (N.J.1985).

The remedies for the breach of an expressed contract are those damages within the contemplation of the parties, including lost wages and other out of pocket losses necessarily attached to the employer's breach. Recovery of personal injury or punitive damages is unlikely.

## § 1.04  Harassment and Common Law Torts

Fondling or grabbing a person without her consent, or attempting such conduct, is the common law tort of assault and battery. Holding an employee against her will or blocking her exit from a room is false imprisonment. *Pease v. Alford Photo Industries, Inc.* (W.D.Tenn.1987). Conduct designed to belittle or humiliate an employee, such as racial harassment, which results in the employee suffering significant emotional injury, is the tort of intentional infliction of emotional harm. *Ford v. Revlon, Inc.* (Ariz.1987). A right of privacy may be invaded by undue intrusions into a worker's private life. Tortious invasions permit one to recover compensatory damages for medical costs, pain, suffering, and humiliation, and punitive damages for malicious conduct. *Pease v. Alford Photo Industries, Inc.,* supra.

# CHAPTER 2

# LABOR RELATIONS STATUTES

## § 2.01  Employer Discrimination

The Railway Labor Act, 45 U.S.C.A. § 151, (RLA) and the National Labor Relations Act, 29 U.S.C.A. § 151, (NLRA) protect the rights of workers to organize, engage in collective bargaining, and use economic weapons ("concerted activity for mutual aid and protection"), and prohibit discrimination because of membership or non-membership in a labor organization. Discrimination by the *employer* on the basis of race, sex, national origin, age, or disability is not prohibited by the labor relations statutes, nor does such discrimination necessarily interfere with the right of employees to engage in the concerted activity which is protected by these statutes. *Jubilee Mfg. Co.* (NLRB 1973). However, as discrimination at the workplace is a condition of employment, workers who *protest* such discrimination through handbills, strikes, or peaceful pickets are engaging in "concerted activity" which is protected against employer discrimination. *New Negro Alliance v. Sanitary Grocery Co.* (S.Ct.1938). To be protected, however, such protests must be peaceful, cannot demand that the employer take illegal action, cannot violate a collective bargaining agree-

7

ment, and cannot undermine the position of the exclusive bargaining representative. *Emporium Capwell Co. v. Western Addition Community Organization* (S.Ct.1975). Rights under the NLRA are enforced exclusively by the National Labor Relations Board. Airline and railway employees covered by the RLA enforce their rights directly in federal court.

## § 2.02  Union Discrimination:  The Duty of Fair Representation

In *Steele v. Louisville & Nashville R. Co.* (S.Ct. 1944) a certified labor union negotiated a collective bargaining contract with an employer that led to the discharge of black employees. Notwithstanding the absence of language in the statute prohibiting race discrimination, the Court held that bargaining representatives have an *implied* duty of fair representation which extends to all members of the bargaining unit, not just to union members. This duty obligates the certified union "to serve all members without hostility or discrimination toward any, to exercise its discretion in good faith and honesty." *Vaca v. Sipes* (S.Ct.1967). It prohibits the union from proposing or accepting contract clauses with racial, ethnic, or gender distinctions, and prohibits discriminatory administration of neutral contract provisions, as, for example, refusing to process grievances of women or minorities. *NLRB v. International Longshoremen's Ass'n, Local 1581, AFL–CIO* (5th Cir.1974). Unions segregated by race or sex, or unions which have exclusionary admissions policies violate their duty of fair representation. *NLRB v. Local No. 106, Glass Bottle Blowers Ass'n, AFL–CIO* (6th Cir.1975).

Breach of the union's duty of fair representation can be remedied through a damage and injunction suit in federal district court or through unfair labor practice proceedings before the National Labor Relations Board.

## § 2.03  Bargaining and the Collective Bargaining Agreement

The union's duty of fair representation requires it to protest discriminatory conduct by the employer and to propose contractual provisions that prohibit such discrimination. *Local Union No. 12, United Rubber, Cork, Linoleum and Plastic Workers v. NLRB* (5th Cir.1966). The employer's statutory duty to bargain in good faith over "wages, hours, terms and conditions of employment" requires it to negotiate over union proposals to eliminate discrimination and to provide the union with statistical information concerning salaries, hiring practices, and the composition of the work force. *Detroit Edison Co. v. NLRB* (S.Ct.1979). Consequently, most collective bargaining contracts expressly prohibit discrimination in language that mirrors that of federal anti-discrimination statutes. Even where they do not, contractual provisions routinely prohibit discharge except for "good cause" and require that promotions be based on a combination of seniority and merit. Decisions premised on race, sex, or ethnic origin violate such general prohibitions.

## § 2.04  Enforcement of the Collective Bargaining Agreement

### a.  Union Enforcement

Collective bargaining agreements uniformly contain grievance arbitration machinery. Enforcement is initiated when the affected employee files a grievance. The union, however, has exclusive authority to invoke the arbitration provisions of the agreement, and it conducts the proceedings before the arbitrator on behalf of the employee. The arbitrator's award is reviewed by the courts applying federal standards, *Textile Workers Union v. Lincoln Mills of Alabama* (S.Ct.1957), and it will be enforced by the courts if the award "draws its essence" from the collective agreement. The award will not be set aside simply because the court disagrees with the arbitrator's decision or because the award conflicts with the court's general view of "public policy." *United Paperworkers Intern. Union v. Misco* (S.Ct.1987).

An arbitrator's award in a case fairly presented by the union precludes litigation by the employee of contract claims. However, the arbitrator's award will not preclude the employee's enforcement of rights granted by federal fair employment *statutes,* even if the statutory rights depend upon facts previously resolved by the arbitrator. *Alexander v. Gardner–Denver Co.* (S.Ct.1974).

### b.  Individual Enforcement

The employee has no power to judicially enforce collective bargaining contract rights if the union, consistent with its duty of fair representation, elects not to seek arbitration of an employee's grievance. Merely because the employer breached the contract does not in itself establish that the union breached its duty in refusing to invoke arbitration. *Vaca v. Sipes* (S.Ct.1967). However, if the union's refusal to invoke arbitration or its conduct of the arbitration hearing breaches its duty of fair representation, the employee is freed by the union's illegal conduct to enforce the contract provisions against the employer. *Hines v. Anchor Motor Freight, Inc.* (S.Ct.1976).

# CHAPTER 3

# HISTORY AND OVERVIEW OF EMPLOYMENT DISCRIMINATION STATUTES AND PROGRAMS

## § 3.01 Title VII of the Civil Rights Act of 1964

There is no single "employment discrimination" statute. Federal employment discrimination law is a patchwork of statutes and one major executive order. Each statute prohibits specific forms of invidious discrimination. Title VII of the Civil Rights Act of 1964, 42 U.S.C.A. § 2000e et seq. (Title VII), is, however, the centerpiece of employment discrimination law. It proscribes discrimination because of race, color, religion, sex (which includes pregnancy), and national origin, and it reaches employers, labor organizations, and employment agencies. Judicial constructions of Title VII are usually applied to other employment discrimination statutes.

Title VII is but one title of the omnibus civil rights bill of 1964. Each title was essentially a separate piece of legislation with a distinct legislative history. Title VII's path through Congress was unusual. The bill first passed the House of Representatives. The Senate took up the House

12

version of the bill on the Senate floor, without reference to committee. During the debate numerous amendments and provisos were offered, many of them products of behind-the-scenes compromise. Debate and interpretative memoranda read into the record provide the main source of legislative intent. The Senate's version of the largely rewritten House bill was not referred to a Conference Committee. Rather it was sent directly to the House floor where it was enacted without amendment. Title VII thus produced no Senate hearings or reports and no Conference Committee report.

Title VII was extensively amended in 1972. The Equal Employment Opportunity Commission (EEOC), the agency charged with enforcing the statute, was authorized to file judicial actions. Time limitations were lengthened, coverage was extended to include public employers, and a number of significant "housekeeping" clarifications were added, particularly in the area of religious discrimination. The Act was amended in 1978 to add a definition of "sex" that included "pregnancy and childbirth."

Reacting to Court decisions of the 1988–89 term, Congress passed extensive amendments in the Civil Rights Act of 1991. The amendments, among other things, redefine the burdens in disparate impact cases, prohibit discriminatory adjustment of test scores, limit challenges to judicially affirmed affirmative action plans, allow jury trials, define the time to challenge seniority systems, and allow damages for intentional discrimination. (Appendix)

## § 3.02 The Age Discrimination in Employment Act of 1967 (ADEA)

Age discrimination against individuals over age 40 is proscribed by the Age Discrimination in Employment Act, 29 U.S.C.A. § 621 et seq. (ADEA). While similar in wording to Title VII, the ADEA has some defenses and provisos uniquely applicable to age discrimination. Coverage is similar to Title VII, but the ADEA has distinct enforcement mechanisms and, unlike Title VII, allows the recovery of liquidated damages.

During the debate on Title VII, "age" was proposed as a protected class. The amendment was rejected, but Congress directed the Secretary of Labor to suggest legislation to remedy discrimination based on age. That 1965 report formed the basis of the ADEA.

The ADEA draws its operative language from Title VII, and thus was intended to receive similar judicial construction. The administrative responsibilities that the original Act vested in the Secretary of Labor were transferred by the 1978 administrative reorganization to the EEOC. Thus, pre–1978 ADEA cases brought by the government were instituted by the "Secretary."

Amendments in 1974 extended coverage to governmental employers. Amendments in 1978 expressly prohibited mandatory retirement and extended the protected age class from age 65 to age 70. Technical amendments in 1982 and 1984 attempted to reconcile the ADEA obligations for employee benefits with employer obligations under Medicare and Medicaid. Amendments in 1986 eliminated the age 70 upper age limit on protection. Pre–1986 cases which discuss the protected age class of 40–70 must be read in light of the 1986 amendment. Special provisions in the 1986 amendments allowed states to retain age rules for hiring and retirement of police and fire fighters.

Amendments in 1990 required age-based differences in benefit plans to be justified by their costs, clarified standards by which employees could be granted severance pay as part of early retirement programs, and established standards for waiver of age discrimination claims. A 1991 amendment made procedural changes.

## § 3.03  The Americans With Disabilities Act of 1990 and The Rehabilitation Act of 1973

Discrimination against individuals with physical or mental disabilities is prohibited by two statutes: the Rehabilitation Act, 29 U.S.C.A. §§ 706, 791–794; and the Americans With Disabilities Act, 42 U.S.C.A. § 12101 et seq. (ADA). Coverage of the Rehabilitation Act is limited to government employers, recipients of federal financial assistance, and federal contractors. The ADA provides protections similar to the Rehabilitation Act, but will cover all entities subject to Title VII.

The Rehabilitation Act was amended in 1978 to more clearly delineate the protections against employment discrimination. The Civil Rights Restoration Act of 1987, PL 100–259, expanded coverage of this and similar program-coverage statutes (such as Title VI of the 1964 Civil Rights Act, and Title IX of the Education Act) by re-defining "program or activity" to include not just the program receiving the federal funding, but the entire corporation, organization, or entity receiving the federal financial assistance. The 1987 Act also eliminated Eleventh Amendment immunity for state governments.

The Americans With Disabilities Act of 1990 (ADA) is an independent statute, not an amendment to the Rehabilitation Act, which reaches employment, public services, public accommodations, and telecommunications. Title I, which addresses employment, prohibits discrimination against persons with disabilities by employers subject to Title VII. Procedures and remedies of Title VII are adopted to enforce these provisions. While the ADA utilizes more expansive language in defining the scope of protection and the extent of required accommodation of disabilities than does the Rehabilitation Act, the legislative history of the ADA indicates that the purpose of this language was to mirror Title VII and to adopt judicial constructions given the more general language of the earlier Rehabilitation Act. The Rehabilitation Act was not repealed by the ADA.  As to employment, the ADA will become effective on July 26, 1992, with full coverage extended on July 26, 1994.

## § 3.04  The Immigration Reform and Control Act of 1986

Citizenship discrimination against American citizens and defined "intending citizens" and national origin discrimination by employers not covered by Title VII is proscribed in the Immigration Reform and Control Act, 8 U.S.C.A. § 1324B.  This Act covers employers of more than three employees, and is administered by a Special Counsel in the Department of Justice utilizing administrative fact-finding procedures vastly different from those of Title VII and the ADEA.

Immigration reform in the early 1980s focused on stopping the flow of illegal aliens into the United States by making it illegal for employers to hire aliens not authorized to work in the United States. Civil rights organizations feared that if employers were punished for hiring illegal aliens, employers would refuse to hire all aliens, which Title VII permitted, and notwithstanding Title VII's proscriptions against national origin discrimination, employers might refuse to consider applicants who had non-Anglo names or a "foreign" appearance. To guard against such overreaction, the Act makes it an illegal "immigration related practice" to discriminate against applicants on the basis of "national origin" or on the basis of "citizenship" for persons who are citizens or "intending citizens" of the United States.

## § 3.05 The Civil Rights Act of 1866, 42 U.S.C.A. § 1981

Race discrimination in the employment "contract" is proscribed by the 1866 Civil Rights Act, 42 U.S.C.A. § 1981. Enacted immediately after the Civil War, this statute was designed to grant to newly freed slaves basic civil rights, such as the right to contract and the right to purchase, hold, and sell property. The portion of the Act now codified at 42 U.S.C.A. § 1981 provides that "all persons * * * shall have the same right * * * to make and enforce contracts * * * as is enjoyed by white citizens * * *." While this prohibition overlaps with Title VII, the 1866 Act has broader coverage, allows more extensive monetary remedies, and is enforced through private judicial remedies without the administrative prerequisites imposed on Title VII plaintiffs.

The 1866 Act was recodified in the 1870s soon after ratification of the Fourteenth Amendment, which granted against state action the rights of due process and equal protection of the laws. For nearly 100 years it was assumed that this codification made § 1981 applicable only to governmental actions. By the 1970s, well after the effective date of Title VII, the Supreme Court held that § 1981 was enacted pursuant to power granted by the Thirteenth Amendment, which abolished slavery, and was thus applicable to private refusals to contract; "state action" was not required to assert a claim under the 1866 Act. *Runyon v. McCrary* (S.Ct.1976). Moreover, the Court held that § 1981 applied to employment "contracts" and was not impliedly repealed or amended by Title VII. *Johnson v. Railway Express Agency, Inc.* (S.Ct.1975).

Congress has rejected proposals to repeal or limit the application of § 1981 or to make Title VII the exclusive remedy in employment discrimination cases. However, a Supreme Court decision holding that § 1981 did not apply to "post formation" discrimination, such as racial harassment, prompted legislative reform in the 1991 Civil Rights Act. This amendment makes the Act applicable not only to the "making" of contracts but also to "the performance, modification, termination, and the enjoyment of all benefits, privileges, terms and conditions of the contractual relationship."

## § 3.06 The Equal Pay Act of 1963 (EPA)

The first modern employment discrimination statute was the Equal Pay Act of 1963, 29 U.S.C.A. § 206(d) (EPA). Inspired by the "equal pay" practices of the War Labor Board of World War II, the EPA was enacted as an amendment to the Fair Labor Standards Act, a statute regulating minimum wages, overtime, and child labor. The EPA imposes an obligation on employers to provide "equal pay" for men and women who perform "equal work" within an establishment unless the difference in pay is based on a seniority or merit system or on some other "factor other than sex." The EPA thus provides an alternative to Title VII for protection against sex-based pay discrimination. Unlike Title VII, however, its remedies include statutory liquidated damages, and it may be privately enforced without administrative prerequisites.

The statute charged the Secretary of Labor with administering the Fair Labor Standards Act. In 1978 enforcement responsibilities for the EPA were transferred by executive reorganization to the EEOC. For this reason pre–1978 cases refer to enforcement by the "Secretary."

## § 3.07  Executive Order 11246

Executive Order 11246, 29 Fed.Reg. 2477, requires employers with federal service and supply contracts and employers performing federally financed construction to undertake "affirmative action." The Order is implemented by regulations from the Department of Labor. 41 CFR Parts 60–1 and 60–2. The affirmative action obligation, in addition to prohibiting discrimination on the basis of race, sex, and national origin, which largely duplicates Title VII, imposes on contracting employers an additional obligation to undertake a "utilization analysis" to determine the extent to which qualified women and minorities are underrepresented in the various job categories of the employer's work force in proportion to their general availability in the relevant job market, and to adopt a written plan to remedy any underutilization. The plan shall include reasonable numerical goals and a timetable for reaching each goal, and generally it includes a commitment by the employer to use hiring ratios based on race, sex, or national origin in order to reach the stated goals.

The employer's contractual obligation to make good faith efforts to reach the goals stated in its affirmative action plan is enforced by the federal contracting agency through suits enforcing or terminating the government contract or, in extreme cases, through administrative action before the Department of Labor to debar the employer from future federal contracts. As a general proposition there is no private judicial remedy. The aggrieved individual may file an administrative complaint with the Department of Labor.

The first executive order requiring government contractors to take "affirmative action" was issued during World War II. Similar orders were repromulgated by successive Presidents. These orders remained largely hortatory until the early 1970s when regulations adopted by the Department of Labor for the first time defined "affirmative action" to impose a duty on government contractors to remedy underutilization of women and minorities through numerical hiring goals tied to specific timetables. As E.O. 11246 and its implementing regulations are products of executive action, the program may be revoked or amended by executive action without Congressional approval. Notwithstanding the rhetoric of the Reagan–Bush administrations condemning "quotas," neither President has exercised his power to revoke or amend the program.

The constitutionality of the program has been sustained as being within the power of the Executive to determine the terms and conditions under which the Executive will do business. *Contractors Ass'n of Eastern Pa. v. Secretary of Labor* (3d Cir.1971).

# CHAPTER 4

## COVERAGE AND SCOPE OF THE MAJOR EMPLOYMENT DIS-CRIMINATION STATUTES

### § 4.01 Title VII, the ADEA, and the ADA

*a. Generally*

Title VII, the ADEA, and the Americans With Disabilities Act follow identical theories of coverage. Individuals are not covered; only persons who are "employers," "labor organizations," or "employment agencies" are covered. Whether a person is an "employer" subject to these statutes depends almost exclusively upon the number of its employees. A union is a covered "labor organization" if it represents or is seeking to represent employees of a defined "employer" and if the union has a sufficient number of members. Employment agency coverage is based upon securing employees for an "employer."

*b. "Employer"*

*(1) "Person Affecting Commerce".* An "employer" must be a "person" in an industry "affecting commerce." "Person" includes any legal entity. "Affecting commerce" is the outer limit of congressional regulatory power. Any person with the requisite number of employees surely will "affect commerce." *EEOC v. Ratliff* (9th Cir.1990). There is no charitable organization exception to coverage.

*(2) Number of Employees.* To be a covered "employer" Title VII requires the person to have fifteen or more employees. The ADEA requires *twenty* employees. As of July 26, 1992, the ADA will cover persons with *twenty-five* or more employees. On July 26, 1994 that number will be reduced to fifteen, the same as Title VII.

*(3) Number of Days.* The minimum number of employees must be employed for "each working day for twenty or more calendar weeks in the current or previous year." 42 U.S.C.A. § 2000e–(b). The twenty weeks need not be consecutive. If a total of twenty weeks of employment within the year are satisfied, all employment decisions in that *and the next* calendar year are covered. Employees will be counted for purposes of determining "employer" coverage only if employed on "each working day" of a week. *Zimmerman v. North Am. Signal Co.* (7th Cir.1983). Thus, casual or part-time employees are protected by the Acts, but they will not be counted for the purpose of determining whether an employer is covered by the statutes.

*(4) State and Local Governments.*  State and local government agencies that employ the necessary number of employees are "employers" subject to the same obligations as private employers.  *EEOC v. Monclova Township* (6th Cir.1990).  "Employee" is defined to exclude persons elected to public office and those personal staff members who work in policy-making positions.  Such high level, policymakers are not counted for the purpose of determining the coverage of the governmental office.  However, the 1991 Civil Rights Act specifically protects these employees against discrimination.  Appendix, § 321.  *Teneyuca v. Bexar County* (5th Cir.1985).

Coverage of state and local governments and the authorization of private suits against state agencies is constitutional.  *Fitzpatrick v. Bitzer* (S.Ct. 1976).

*(5) The Federal Government.*  Although the federal government is excluded from the definition of "employer," the statutes prohibit federal government discrimination.  Since the federal government is not an "employer," procedures and remedies applicable to "employers" are not applicable to the federal government.  Special procedures and remedies are provided.  Coverage was limited to the executive department and to judicial and legislative departments subject to competitive civil service.  The 1991 Civil Rights Act extends coverage to congressional employees and presidential appointees.

Civilian employees of military departments are covered, but as military service is a relationship other than "employment," military personnel decisions are outside the scope of these laws. *Roper v. Department of the Army* (2d Cir.1987).

(6) *Bona Fide Membership Clubs.* Excluded from the Title VII and ADA definition of "employer" are bona fide private membership clubs (other than labor organizations) which are exempt from taxation under the Internal Revenue Code. In addition to tax exempt status, a "club" must have a defined social or recreational purpose or promote a common literary, scientific, or political objective, and demand meaningful conditions of membership. Credit unions, nursing homes, and hospitals do not satisfy this definition. *Quijano v. University Fed. Credit Union* (5th Cir.1980). Athletic clubs and country clubs may. *Hudson v. Charlotte Country Club, Inc.* (W.D.N.C.1982). The ADEA has no expressed exclusion for membership clubs.

(7) *Indian Tribes.* Indian tribes are excluded from the Title VII definition of "employer." This exclusion applies to the semi-sovereign political entity and to commercial activities undertaken by the tribe. *Dille v. Council of Energy Resource Tribes* (10th Cir.1986). While the ADEA does not expressly exclude tribes from coverage, the Act cannot be applied to a tribe's sovereign activity. *EEOC v. Cherokee Nation* (10th Cir.1989).

(8) *Religious Organizations.* Religious organizations with the requisite number of employees *are* defined "employers." However, Title VII allows

religions and religious educational institutions *to hire* on the basis of *religion* or religious belief and practices. 42 U.S.C.A. §§ 2000e–1 and e–2(d)(2). This exemption for religious discrimination by religious organizations is applicable to *all activities of the religion,* including secular enterprises. For example, a religious organization can discriminate on the basis of religion in hiring and retaining employees at a secular gymnasium, and the exemption does not violate the First Amendment's prohibition against the "establishment" of religion. *Corporation of Presiding Bishop v. Amos* (S.Ct. 1987).

The prohibition against race, sex, national origin, age, and disability discrimination creates tension between the statutes and the First Amendment prohibitions on governmental infringement of the "free exercise" of religion. A religion's selection, assignment, dismissal, or pay of its ministers, priests, leaders, rabbis, or teachers—activities that go to the core of the religious practices—cannot be challenged, because to do so would inject enforcement agencies into the religion in violation of the First Amendment. *Scharon v. St. Luke's Episcopal Presbyterian Hospitals* (8th Cir.1991). On the other hand race, sex, national origin, or age discrimination in a religion's secular activity or in the religion's treatment of support staff at religious institutions, such as seminaries or religious publishing houses, violates the Acts, and enforcement of the Acts will not violate the Constitution. *EEOC v. Southwestern Baptist Theological Seminary* (5th Cir.1981).

Secular employers, who are not themselves "religions" but who desire to discriminate in favor of those with similar beliefs, cannot claim the statutory exemption accorded religions. Failure of the statute to accord exemption to secular employers, thus making them fully subject to Title VII, does not violate their First Amendment right to the "free exercise" of religion. *EEOC v. Townley Engineering & Mfg. Co.* (9th Cir.1988).

*(9) Extra–Territorial Application.* The ADEA was made applicable to American employers abroad, including foreign corporations controlled by American employers, in their treatment of American citizens unless otherwise required by the law of the host nation. Title VII had no similar language giving it extra-territorial application, a claim of national origin discrimination by a citizen employed by an American company in Saudi Arabia was rejected. *EEOC v. Arabian American Oil Co.* (S.Ct.1991). The 1991 Amendments give Title VII extra-territorial application identical to the ADEA.

c. *"Labor Organization"*

A "labor organization" is an association which exists in whole or in part to deal with employers concerning grievances, labor disputes, and terms or conditions of employment. To be covered the "labor organization" must be "engaged in an industry affecting commerce" which occurs if the union maintains a hiring hall, or has fifteen or more members (twenty-five under the ADEA) and is certified or recognized by a defined "employer" as the exclusive bargaining representative, is actively seeking to represent such employees, or charters an organization which represents or seeks to represent employees. Most organizations that fall within the conception of a labor union will be covered.

Unions representing employees of state and local governments and federal executive departments are covered by the statutes, even though they may not literally fall within the definition which requires that the employer be in an industry "affecting commerce." *Jennings v. American Postal Workers Union* (8th Cir.1982).

### d.  *"Employment Agency"*

An "employment agency" is "any person regularly undertaking with or without compensation to procure employees for an employer * * *." An "employment agency" need not itself have a minimum number of employees, but it will not be covered unless it procures employees for a defined "employer." State employment services and even civil service personnel boards, if they place persons with private employers or other agencies within the government, are covered. *Dumas v. Mount Vernon* (5th Cir.1980).

In addition to the statutory elements, the entity must meet an implicit requirement that it is viewed as an employment agency within the "generally accepted sense of the term." Help-wanted ads attempt to procure employees for employers, but newspapers which print them are not generally accepted as "employment agencies." *Brush v. San Francisco Newspaper Printing Co.* (N.D.Cal. 1970). Colleges are academic institutions, not "employment agencies," *Cannon v. University of Chicago* (7th Cir.1976), although placement office activities may meet the conception. *Kaplowitz v. University of Chicago* (N.D.Ill.1974). Licensing authorities and professional associations are not "employment agencies" unless they perform placement services. *George v. New Jersey Bd. of Veterinary Medical Examiners* (3d Cir.1986).

## § 4.02 Coverage of the Equal Pay Act

### a. *Traditional Employee–Based Coverage*

Equal Pay Act (EPA) coverage is coextensive with coverage of the Fair Labor Standards Act (FLSA). Without regard to the activity of the employer or the number of employees, any employee "engaged in commerce" or engaged in the "production of goods for commerce," which includes activity "closely related or directly essential to the production of goods for commerce," is covered.

"Engaged in commerce" includes employees participating in the actual movement of interstate commerce, such as truck drivers, pilots, flight attendants, communications operators, power line and pipeline workers. Persons who directly assist in the movement of commerce by repairing vehicles, patching pipelines, and maintaining roads are "engaged in commerce," as are local ambulance and wrecker drivers. Persons who create instrumentalities of commerce by building links in interstate highways or by constructing transportation terminals, airports, docks, and transmission lines are "engaged in commerce."

"Production of goods for commerce" includes all processes directly contributing to goods or products that will enter the interstate market; providing an ingredient, supplying necessary power, or making the packaging for a product destined for interstate shipment. A night watchman at a local junkyard was engaged in the "production of goods for commerce" because a small percentage of the junk that he protected from pilfering was sold locally to a steel manufacturer which, in turn, used the junk as an ingredient in steel ultimately sold on an interstate market. *Mitchell v. Jaffe* (5th Cir.1958).

### b. Enterprise Coverage

Coverage of FLSA also is provided to *all* employees of an "enterprise engaged in commerce." An enterprise is "engaged in commerce" if it has two or more employees engaged in commerce, producing goods for commerce, or handling goods that have been moved in commerce. In addition, regardless of its size, the enterprise will be covered if it is a government agency, is involved in construction or laundering, or operates a school or hospital. If the enterprise does not fall into any of the above categories it will be covered if it has annual sales or "business done" of at least $362,500. Thus, most employers of more than minimal economic size will have *all* of their employees covered by the EPA.

### c. Exemptions

FLSA has a number of exemptions largely applicable to defined types of businesses (e.g., small retail operations, employees of small agricultural enterprises, seasonal amusements, fishing, foreign flag ships). 29 U.S.C.A. § 213(a). The exemption for professional, administrative, and executive employees under the wage-hour provisions of FLSA is *inapplicable* to the equal pay provisions of EPA.

### d. Governmental Employees

Public agencies, including federal executive departments, are one of the specified industries defined to be an "enterprise engaged in commerce." Excluded from the definition of "employee" are persons who serve on the personal staff of elected office holders, are appointed by elected officials to policy-making positions, or who serve as immediate advisors to elected officials. 29 U.S.C.A. § 206(e)(2)(c)

The constitutionality of EPA coverage of state and local governments was confirmed by *Garcia v. San Antonio Metro. Transit Auth.* (S.Ct.1985).

## e. Labor Organizations

FLSA coverage provisions, because they are concerned solely with minimum pay and overtime compensation, do not mention labor organizations. In contrast, the EPA provides: "No labor organization representing employees of an employer shall cause or attempt to cause such employer to discriminate against an employee in violation of the [equal pay provisions]."  29 U.S.C.A. § 206(d)(2). The enforcement provisions of the FLSA, which must be used to enforce the EPA, provide, however, that "[a]ny *employer* who violates the provisions * * * shall be liable to employees * * *."  Because no provision is made for a private suit to collect back wages against a union, *private actions* against unions are not available under the EPA.  *Northwest Airlines, Inc. v. Transport Workers Union* (D.C.Cir.1979).  There is no limitation on EEOC suits against unions.

## § 4.03  Coverage of the Immigration Reform and Control Act and the 1866 Civil Rights Act

Coverage of the Immigration Act is based upon Congress' power to regulate immigration, and thus contact with commerce or business size of the employer is not important.  The Act proscribes discrimination by "a person or other entity," but exempts any person or entity with three or fewer employees.  The proscriptions against "national origin" discrimination apply only to employers that are not covered by Title VII.

The 1866 Civil Rights Act implements the Thirteenth Amendment, and similarly has no "affecting commerce" requirement for coverage, either in terms of economic size or number of workers. The Act prohibits "all persons" from discriminating in the making or enforcing of contracts.

## § 4.04 Coverage of E.O. 11246 and the Rehabilitation Act

E.O. 11246 applies to employers with federal government service and supply contracts and employers who perform federally financed construction. The fact that the government contract was unknown to the employer (as in the case of a subcontractor) or unavoidable (as in the case of a utility) does not remove coverage. *United States v. New Orleans Public Service* (5th Cir.1977).

The Rehabilitation Act covers federal government employees, employers with government contracts, and public or private entities which receive federal financial aid or support. The number of employees or contact with interstate commerce is not relevant. Coverage is not limited to programs that provide employment. The entity receiving the aid, not just the specific program being aided, is subject to the Act. For example, a bank participating in a loan guarantee program of the Small Business Administration is covered in regard to its employment activity.  *Moore v. Sun Bank of North Florida, N.A.* (11th Cir.1991).

## § 4.05   General Prohibitions and Scope of the Statutes

### a.  *Protected Classes*

"No matter how medieval a firm's practices, no matter how high-handed its decisional process, no matter how mistaken the firm's managers," if the discrimination is not "because of": (1) race, (2) color, (3) religion, (4) sex, (5) national origin, (6) citizenship, (7) age, or (8) disability, the law does not interfere.  *Pollard v. Rea Magnet Wire Co.* (7th Cir.1987).

### b.  *Discriminatory Acts*

*(1) "Employers"* may not "fail or refuse to hire, discharge, or otherwise discriminate against any individual with respect to compensation, terms, conditions, or privileges of employment" nor "limit, segregate, or classify employees or applicants for employment in any way which would tend to deprive any individual of employment opportunities or otherwise adversely affect his status as an employee."  These Acts "are not limited to 'economic' or 'tangible' discrimination * * * but strike at the entire spectrum of disparate treatment * * *."  *Meritor Savings Bank, FSB v. Vinson* (S.Ct.1986).

Discrimination by employers must relate to "employment."  An employer's action that does not address or affect employment is beyond the scope of the Title VII, the ADA, or the ADEA. For example, the decision to enter into an independent contract for the purchase of goods or services (such as insurance, professional advice, car repair, or building construction) is not "employment." To determine whether a person performing services is an "independent contractor," and thus not subject to these statutes, the courts examine the economic realities of the relationship in light of the common law principles of agency. Agency law emphasizes the employer's right to control the actions of the employees; the more control over the means and manner by which a person performs job duties, the more likely the relationship will be "employment." Important also is the opportunity of the worker to secure entrepreneurial profit from planning and initiative; whether the worker or the "employer" supplies the tools and materials; which party sets the time, place and manner of performance; whether the worker has the ability to hire and direct others; and who is responsible for taxes and insurance. *Martin v. United Way of Erie County* (3d Cir.1987).

Because 42 U.S.C.A. § 1981 regulates discrimination in contracting, the distinction between employment and an independent contract does not affect coverage of § 1981.

Eligibility to purchase corporate stock and election of corporate directors are outside the scope of the Acts. *EEOC v. Dowd & Dowd, Ltd.* (7th Cir. 1984). Executives are "employees" of the corporation, however, and providing stock as compensation to employees is a term of employment which cannot be discriminatorily allocated. Moreover, *Price Waterhouse v. Hopkins* (S.Ct.1989) held that "decisions pertaining to advancement to a partnership are, of course, subject to challenge under Title VII." The courts are divided on whether reorganization of a partnership or professional corporation in which former partners are excluded is "entrepreneurial" and thus outside the scope of the Acts. *Fountain v. Metcalf, Zima & Co., P.A.,* (11th Cir. 1991).

A prisoner, even though working in a prison industry, is not an "employee" for purposes of the statutes; the relationship is one of incarceration. *Williams v. Meese* (10th Cir.1991). Title VII and the ADEA do not reach decisions by schools in the selection or retention of students, even if the student secures a stipend in return for services. *Pollack v. Rice University* (S.D.Tex.1982). (Education discrimination for institutions receiving federal financial assistance is reached by Title VI of the 1964 Civil Rights Act, 42 U.S.C.A. § 2000d; Title IX of the Education Amendments of 1972, 20 U.S.C.A. § 1681; and the Age Discrimination Act of 1975, 42 U.S.C.A. § 6101. Denial of admission on the basis of race also violates 42 U.S.C.A. § 1981.)

*(2) "Labor Organization"* may not "exclude or expel from its membership, * * * limit, segregate, or classify its membership or applicants, or classify or fail or refuse to refer for employment any individual in a way which would deprive or tend to deprive any individual of employment opportunities." 42 U.S.C.A. § 2000e–2(c)(1) and (2). This prohibits discrimination in the union's internal affairs, in its referral of individuals for work, and in its administration of collective bargaining agreements. Discriminatory treatment need not deny individuals economic benefits. Any segregation based on protected classes is illegal. *Lutcher v. Musicians Union Local 47* (9th Cir.1980). Finally, it is illegal for unions to cause or attempt to cause an employer to violate the Acts. 42 U.S.C.A. § 2000e–2(c)(3).

The Landrum–Griffin Act, 29 U.S.C.A. § 401 et seq., also grants broad rights of union members to participate in the affairs of the union, including free speech and assembly, and it broadly prohibits arbitrary treatment of members by the union.

*(3) "Employment Agencies"* may not "fail or refuse to refer for employment, or otherwise discriminate, * * * or classify * * * any individual [because of race, sex, national origin, religion, age, or disability.]" 42 U.S.C.A. 2000e–2(b). This prohibits honoring discriminatory requests by employers or even maintaining segregated files.

*(4) Notices and Advertisements.* The Acts prohibit covered entities from printing, publishing, or causing to be published notices "indicating any preference, limitation, specification, or discrimination" based on membership in a protected class unless such preference is based on a bona fide occupational qualification. 42 U.S.C.A. § 2000e–3(b).

# CHAPTER 5

# THE EQUAL EMPLOYMENT OPPORTUNITY COMMISSION (EEOC)

## § 5.01 The Commission and Its Functions

The agency charged with administration and enforcement of Title VII, the ADEA, the ADA, and the EPA is the Equal Employment Opportunity Commission (EEOC), a five person, presidentially appointed independent commission. The EEOC has an office of General Counsel charged with litigating on behalf of the EEOC. Regional offices of the EEOC are located throughout the country.

Persons who desire to enforce rights granted by Title VII, the ADEA, and the ADA must file timely charges with a regional office of the EEOC. The EEOC is directed to investigate charges, and "[i]f the Commission determines after such investigation that there is reasonable cause to believe that the charge is true, the Commission shall endeavor to eliminate any such alleged unlawful employment practice by informal methods of conference, conciliation, and persuasion."

Upon the filing of a timely charge, and after the failure of conciliation, the EEOC may file suit against non-governmental employers. If the EEOC elects not to file suit, the charging party is free to file a private judicial action. The EEOC may formally intervene in such litigation. The EEOC has authority to file suits under the Equal Pay Act without any request or charge being filed by the aggrieved employee. The Attorney General has the exclusive authority to file suit against state and local governmental entities. Public suits against federal agencies are not authorized.

The EEOC is granted broad subpoena powers to investigate charges of discrimination and the power to require covered employers, unions, and employment agencies to maintain records and make periodic reports to the EEOC. Large employers are required to file statistical reports with the EEOC.

The EEOC issues formal interpretative guidelines. Guidelines are not regulations that have the force of law, but are accorded "great deference" by the courts. The EEOC also issues less formal "policy statements" on numerous interpretative and enforcement questions. Guidelines are published in the Code of Federal Regulations (CFR). The ADEA also grants the EEOC power to create through regulation exemptions to the prohibitions of the ADEA.

The EEOC serves as a review tribunal over federal agency determinations of discrimination charges brought within the federal agency. EEOC regulations establish the procedures that each federal agency must follow in reviewing charges of discrimination. Adverse determinations by the agency *may* be appealed by aggrieved employees to the EEOC. The EEOC has the power to overturn final agency actions and order the agency to take appropriate remedial steps. The 1991 Amendments give the EEOC authority to review changes by Presidential appointees.

# CHAPTER 6

# MISCELLANEOUS PROTECTIONS

## § 6.01 Constitutional Protections for Public Employees: Free Speech, Equal Protection, and Due Process of Law

Discrimination by a government employer against a worker or applicant because of the individual's speech, social action, or political association triggers a claim under the First Amendment to the Constitution. *Rankin v. McPherson* (S.Ct. 1987); *Rutan v. Republican Party of Illinois* (S.Ct. 1990).

The Fifth and Fourteenth Amendments also impose on governments an obligation not to take "property" or infringe "liberties" without "due process of law." This imposes a substantive obligation on public employers not to enact rules that unreasonably infringe upon fundamental liberties such as those involving marriage, family, or interstate travel. *Cleveland Bd. of Educ. v. LaFleur* (S.Ct. 1974). Moreover, if the employee has a "legitimate claim of entitlement" to continued employment, the employee cannot be dismissed without the government providing notice of the reasons and a

43

fair opportunity to be heard. *Board of Regents of State Colleges v. Roth* (S.Ct.1972); *Perry v. Sindermann* (S.Ct.1972).

Race, sex, alienage, ethnic origin, and religious discrimination by state and local government employers may be challenged through suits filed under 42 U.S.C.A. § 1983. *Ambach v. Norwick* (S.Ct. 1979). Title VII, however, is the exclusive remedy for such complaints against federal employers. *Brown v. General Services Admin.* (S.Ct.1976).

## § 6.02   Veterans and Veterans Preferences

Employers are required to reinstate without penalty persons returning from military service into the positions they would have obtained had their employment not been interrupted by the service. 38 U.S.C.A. § 2021; *Alabama Power Co. v. Davis* (S.Ct.1977). This Act may be enforced by private judicial action.

Veterans of the Vietnam Era may not be discriminated against by employers with significant government contracts in the initial hiring, promotion, training, discharge, or status. There is no private judicial action under this Act; charges are processed through the Veterans Employment Service. 38 U.S.C.A. § 2011.

Title VII specifically preserves statutory veterans preferences from any challenge under Title VII. 42 U.S.C.A. § 2000e–11.

## § 6.03    Polygraph Tests

Except for security officers or positions that involve handling controlled substances, private employers may not require or suggest that an applicant take a lie detector test.  A polygraph test may be given to current employees if: (1) it is given in conjunction with an ongoing investigation of economic loss, (2) the employee had access to the lost property, (3) the employer had reasonable suspicion that the employee was involved, and (4) the employee is provided a statement of the loss and the basis for the employer's suspicion.  The employee may be discharged based on the outcome of the test only if the employer has additional evidence of the employee's guilt.  29 U.S.C.A. § 2001.

## § 6.04    Pension Benefits (ERISA)

The Employee Retirement Income Security Act of 1974 (ERISA), 29 U.S.C.A. § 1001 *et seq.,* prohibits discharge or discrimination by an employer in an effort to interfere with employee benefits, including pensions, or to reduce obligations under pension or health benefit plans.  *Reichman v. Bonsignore, Brignati & Mazzotta P.C.* (2d Cir.1987).  This right may be enforced by private judicial action and is often joined with claims of age discrimination.

## § 6.05    Credit

The Consumer Credit Protection Act, 15 U.S.C.A. § 1674(a), provides that "[n]o employer may discharge an employee by reason that his earnings have been subject to garnishment for any one indebtedness." This Act also limits the use of credit reports in making employment decisions.

The Bankruptcy Act makes it illegal for a private employer to discriminate against an individual who has been a debtor or bankrupt or associated with such a debtor or bankrupt, and it prohibits discharge based on the refusal to pay a discharged or dischargeable debt. 11 U.S.C.A. § 525.

# PART II

# THE CORE OF EMPLOY-MENT DISCRIMINATION LAW: THE BASIS OF LIABILITY

## CHAPTER 7

## FACIAL DISCRIMINATION

### § 7.01  The Nature of Facial Distinctions

The most obvious form of discrimination is a distinction that overtly uses proscribed classifications, as, for example, where an employer admittedly refuses to hire an individual because of his disability, refuses to consider women for certain positions (e.g., guard in a male prison), or will not allow workers over a particular age to transfer jobs. *Trans World Airlines, Inc. v. Thurston* (S.Ct. 1985). Overt or facial classifications are not necessarily illegal. They can be justified by proof that limitation of employment to a particular class is a bona fide occupational qualification (infra, Chapt. 8), or that the distinction was made pursuant to a valid affirmative action plan (infra, Chapt. 9).

## § 7.02 Differing Standards and the "Sex–Plus" Notion

It is facial discrimination to require of one protected class credentials or levels of performance not required of other persons. In *Phillips v. Martin Marietta Corp.* (S.Ct.1971), for example, the employer did not exclude women—indeed 75% of its employees were women—but it refused to employ women with pre-school-aged children; men with pre-school-aged children were not disqualified. The court of appeals held that this was not sex discrimination because "sex" was not the sole basis of the discrimination; rather, the distinction was permissibly based on sex *plus* the neutral factor of pre-school-aged children. The Supreme Court reversed, holding, "[Title VII] * * * requires that persons of like qualifications be given employment opportunities irrespective of their sex. The Court of Appeals therefore erred in * * * permitting one hiring policy for women and another for men." Consequently, it is discriminatory to reject females who are married while imposing no marital requirements on men, *Sprogis v. United Air Lines, Inc.* (7th Cir.1971), or to deny employment opportunities to fertile women that are granted to all males. *International Union, UAW v. Johnson Controls, Inc.* (S.Ct.1991). It is race discrimination for a union to use different standards in determining whether to file grievances on behalf of black workers, even if the union's "leaders were favorably disposed toward minorities" and its decisions were good faith attempts to better serve the workers.

*Goodman v. Lukens Steel Co.* (S.Ct.1987). It is race discrimination for an employer to inquire about the work history or criminal records of black applicants, rejecting those with records, without making similar inquiries of white applicants. *Howard v. Roadway Express, Inc.* (11th Cir.1984).

## § 7.03  Discipline and Discharge for "Good Cause"

A different response to substandard performance or misconduct based upon the race, sex, national origin, religion, age, or disability of the actors is facial discrimination, and is not justified simply because there is "good cause" to discipline the particular worker. In *McDonald v. Santa Fe Trail Transp. Co.* (S.Ct.1976) the employer discharged a white employee for theft while similarly situated black employees were retained. The Court held that:

> While Santa Fe may decide that participation in a theft of cargo may render an employee unqualified for employment, this criterion must be 'applied, alike to members of all races,' * * *. [W]hatever factors the mechanisms of compromise may legitimately take into account in mitigating discipline of some employees, under Title VII race may not be among them.

Therefore, discipline that differs along class lines must be based on relevant differences in the conduct, culpability, or work history of the employees involved. *Green v. Armstrong Rubber Co.* (5th Cir. 1980). Sexual conduct tolerated in one gender or age group cannot be punished when practiced by the other gender or different age groups. *Duchon v. Cajon Co.* (6th Cir.1986).

# CHAPTER 8

# BONA FIDE OCCUPATIONAL QUALIFICATION DEFENSE (BFOQ)

## § 8.01  Generally: The Statutes

Title VII provides:

[I]t shall not be an unlawful employment practice * * * to hire and employ * * * on the basis of his religion, sex, or national origin in those certain instances where religion, sex, or national origin is a bona fide occupational qualification reasonably necessary to the normal operation of that particular business or enterprise.

42 U.S.C.A. § 2000e–2(e)

Because Title VII defines "sex" to include pregnancy, pregnancy distinctions are subject to the defense. "Race" is not allowed as a BFOQ, but racial classifications have been justified by a judicially implied "business necessity" defense similar to the BFOQ. The ADEA has a BFOQ defense similar to Title VII. 29 U.S.C.A. § 623(f)(1). The ADA has no BFOQ provision, but allows exclusion of persons with disabilities if the person, with or without

51

reasonable accommodation, cannot perform "essential" job functions, a concept similar to the BFOQ.

## § 8.02  Elements of the BFOQ Defense

*a.  "Essence"*

The BFOQ applies only "to qualifications that affect an employee's ability to do the job." *International Union, UAW v. Johnson Controls, Inc.* (S.Ct.1991).  Defendant must prove that members of the excluded class cannot safely and effectively perform *essential* job duties.  Inability of the excluded class to perform peripheral job duties will not suffice.  For example, even if females provide a psychologically more soothing atmosphere than would men during an airline flight, "soothing atmosphere" is tangential to the primary duty of safely and efficiently transporting passengers, and thus for the job of flight attendant, the female gender is not a bona fide occupational qualification.  *Diaz v. Pan Am. World Airways, Inc.* (5th Cir.1971).

Concern for the welfare of the employee cannot serve as a BFOQ unless the injury to the employee affects the safety of others.  Title VII rejects the romantic paternalism that denies to women the opportunity to work in mines, in construction, or as truck drivers, prison guards, police officers, or fire fighters simply because the occupation is dirty, dangerous, or strenuous.  *Weeks v. Southern Bell Tel. & Tel. Co.* (5th Cir.1969).

Generally, a BFOQ cannot be based upon customer preference, in that customer expectations do not go to the essence of the ability of the worker to perform the job. Therefore, a man may not be denied the job of airline flight attendant because passengers prefer female attendants. *Diaz v. Pan Am. World Airways,* supra. A woman cannot be denied the job as an oil company executive because customers from certain cultures may not desire to deal with women. *Fernandez v. Wynn Oil Co.* (9th Cir.1981).

This general rule is subject to the qualification that customer preference may ultimately deprive the worker of the ability to perform essential job duties. For example, if the modesty of patients makes intimate care by those of the opposite sex impossible to perform without endangering the health of the patient, gender may be a BFOQ for the job. *Fesel v. Masonic Home of Delaware* (D.Del.1978). When women clients or inmates have suffered abuse from men and would respond better to rehabilitation efforts of women counselors, the female gender may be a BFOQ for such positions. *Torres v. Wisconsin Dept. of Health and Social Services* (7th Cir.1988). The Muslim religion is a BFOQ for the job of transporting pilgrims to holy cities where access is limited to Moslems. *Kern v. Dynalectron Corp.* (N.D.Tex.1983).

"Authenticity", which is a form of customer expectation, can be a basis for a BFOQ. An employer may use male models to display male clothing or utilize actresses for female roles in dramatic productions. While restaurants generally cannot prefer waiters over waitresses, because the "essence" of the job of serving food can be performed equally well by both genders, to insure the "authenticity" of the dining experience an Asian restaurant may prefer Asian servers. 29 CFR § 1604.2.

### b.   *"All or Substantially All"*

Defendant must establish that "all or substantially all" persons in the excluded class cannot perform essential job duties. *Dothard v. Rawlinson* (S.Ct.1977) (Title VII); *Western Air Lines, Inc. v. Criswell* (S.Ct.1985) (ADEA). For example, in a job that requires physical prowess, such as strength, an employer could not exclude women or older workers from the job simply because more women than men lack the physical requirements or because significantly more older workers could not perform. If some women posses the physical qualifications, the employer cannot use class membership as a proxy to excuse individual evaluations of fitness. If some persons in the excluded age group can perform the demands of the job, age cannot be a BFOQ.

### c.   *The "Third Party Risk" Exception to the "All or Substantially All" Requirement*

If some members of the excluded class present a substantial risk to the employer or to third parties, *and* if it is impracticable to eliminate the risk through individual evaluations of fitness, a BFOQ may be asserted. For example, in *Dothard v. Rawlinson* (S.Ct.1977) the Court concluded that women guards in a maximum security, all male prison presented an increased risk that because of their sex they would be attacked by male inmates. The Court emphasized that concern for the female employees could not itself justify a BFOQ, but the Court was satisfied that increased incidents of attacks on women posed a significant risk to the general security of the prison that could be eliminated only by the exclusion of women. On the other hand, a general assertion of "safety" was insufficient to justify mandatory retirement at age 60 of an airline's flight engineers without a showing of increased risks to flight safety that could not be protected against by individual evaluations of each engineer's fitness. *Western Air Lines, Inc. v. Criswell* (S.Ct.1985).

Pregnancy, at some point, limits the physical activity of many women. When the pregnant worker is no longer able to perform essential job duties, based on an individual evaluation of her ability, she may be placed on disability leave. But a presumed physical incapacity of pregnant women cannot justify imposing leave on all pregnant employees absent a showing that all or substantially all pregnant women could not perform the job duties. *Burwell v. Eastern Air Lines, Inc.* (4th Cir.1980). As the pregnancy term progresses the chances increase that a miscarriage would physically incapacitate the woman. If the consequence of such incapacity increases the risk of harm to *third persons,* and individual evaluations of each pregnant woman's likelihood to miscarry are unreliable, the employer may assert non-pregnancy as a BFOQ. Such reasoning has sustained non-pregnancy as a BFOQ for airline flight attendants. *Levin v. Delta Air Lines, Inc.* (5th Cir.1984).

*International Union, UAW v. Johnson Controls, Inc.* (S.Ct.1991), held that an employer's exclusion of fertile women, but not fertile men, could not be justified on grounds that the rule protected the woman's reproductive capacity and the physical welfare of the fetus. The safety qualification is limited to those instances where sex or pregnancy presents a danger to customers or third parties. A fetus carried by the employee is not a "third party" whose safety is essential to the operation of the employer's business, and thus cannot be the basis of a BFOQ.

### d. *"Reasonably Necessary"*

The BFOQ must be "reasonably *necessary* to the normal operation of the particular business." Where there is a reasonable alternative to the exclusion of the class, the exclusion is not "necessary." To illustrate, one essential aspect of the job might only be performed by one gender, as in a prison where the modesty interests of the inmates might require intimate searches by members of the same sex. If intimate duties can be realigned without unduly disrupting the employer's normal business operation or imposing significant hardship to fellow workers, realignment is required. *Hardin v. Stynchcomb* (11th Cir.1982).

The duty to use lesser discriminatory alternatives does not require job restructuring or the imposition of significant burdens on other employees. "[T]itle VII does not require an employer to move a pregnant employee into a new job calling for skills and training not associated with the original employment position." *Levin v. Delta Air Lines, Inc.* (5th Cir.1984).

## § 8.03 "Protective" Legislation

State statutes at one time required employers to "protect" women. Women, by law, could not be employed in certain jobs, such as in mines or in bars, and could not be worked at certain times of the day or for more than a certain number of hours per day or week. Such laws themselves cannot serve as a BFOQ. If the employer's exclusion cannot be justified under the federal BFOQ standards, state laws requiring disparate treatment must fail as violating the "supremacy clause" in Art. I of the Constitution. *Rosenfeld v. Southern Pac. Co.* (9th Cir.1971).

## § 8.04 Race as a "Business Necessity"

"Race" is not included in the BFOQ defense. Nonetheless, there may be occasions where a person of one race cannot perform job duties; for example, a person serving as a police undercover investigator or, in the case of actors or models, where certain racial characteristics may be necessary for "authenticity." Prior to 1992 if an employer could prove the "business necessity" for such a racial qualification, Title VII implicitly allowed its use. *Miller v. Texas State Bd. of Barber Examiners* (5th Cir.1980). Defendant had to prove that the exclusion was "reasonably necessary." For example, even though it is rational to assume that a black recruiter could more effectively recruit minority workers than could a white recruiter, defendant had to prove that being black was "reasonably necessary" to perform the recruiter's job. *Knight v. Nassau County Civil Service Com'n* (2d Cir.1981).

Apparently to insure that a business necessity defense could not be used as a substitute for the BFOQ defense in sex discrimination cases, as some lower courts had held, the Civil Rights Act of 1991 specifically provides: "A demonstration that an employment practice is required by business necessity may not be used as a defense against a claim of intentional discrimination." It is now unclear whether "business necessity" can justify use of necessary racial classifications.

# CHAPTER 9

# AFFIRMATIVE ACTION

## § 9.01 The Definition and Sources of "Affirmative Action"

Affirmative action as it is understood today includes, but goes beyond, outreach attempts to recruit minority applicants, special training programs, and the re-evaluation of the effect of selection devices. It presupposes an undertaking to remedy underutilization of women and minorities through express consideration of race or gender.

Executive Order 11246 imposes such affirmative action obligations on employers with construction contracts financed by the federal government and on employers with significant federal service or supply contracts. Supra, § 3.07.

Employers not subject to E.O. 11246 are not required to undertake affirmative action, even if they have a work force that does not reflect the area population. Indeed, a proviso in Title VII specifically provides that nothing in the Act "shall be interpreted to require the grant of preferential treatment on account of an imbalance which may exist" between an employer's work force "in comparison with the total number or percentage of persons of such race, color, religion, sex, or national origin in the available work force." 42 U.S.C.A. § 2000e–2(j). Nonetheless, social pressure or the threat of litigation has induced many employers to adopt "voluntary" affirmative action programs similar to those imposed on government contractors under E.O. 11246.

Affirmative action is imposed by courts upon employers or unions as a judicial remedy upon a finding that the defendant engaged in a pattern of egregious violations of the law. The legality of judicially ordered affirmative action depends upon an evaluation of the scope of the remedial power granted to courts by Title VII. Infra, § 26.06.

## § 9.02  Legality of Affirmative Action

### a.  *Title VII and the Constitution*

The issue presented is whether an affirmative action plan's facial classifications based on race, sex, and national origin violate the Title VII proscriptions against such discrimination and can be reconciled with the statutory proviso not requiring the grant of "preferential treatment." Moreover, when the affirmative action program is adopted by a state or local government, this "state action" raises the additional question of whether the plan violates the Constitution. When "suspect" classifications, such as race or national origin, are utilized by a government they will be subjected to "strict judicial scrutiny." "There are two prongs to this examination. First, any racial classification 'must be justified by a compelling governmental interest'. Second, the means chosen by the State to effectuate its purpose must be 'narrowly tailored to the achievement of that goal.'" *Wygant v. Jackson Bd. of Educ.* (S.Ct.1986).

### b. The Basic Answer: Steelworkers v. Weber

*United Steelworkers v. Weber* (S.Ct.1979) held that the use of race or national origin in making hiring decisions does not violate Title VII where the decisions were made pursuant to an affirmative action plan that met specified standards. *Weber* involved an employer with few minority workers in skilled trades, which entered into an agreement with the union whereby 50% of the persons admitted into an apprenticeship program would be black until the proportion of black skilled workers at the plant approximated the black population of the area. There had been no judicial finding of racial discrimination. Plaintiff, a white man, was excluded from the program notwithstanding the fact that he had greater seniority than some of the blacks and would have been selected into the program had he been black. The lower courts held that the plaintiff was a victim of racial discrimination. The Supreme Court reversed.

The Court first read the Title VII proviso which disclaims "preferential treatment" based on a racial imbalance as prohibiting only "required" use of race, sex, or national origin; the proviso did not prohibit the "voluntary" use of such factors. As to the prohibitions against "race" discrimination, the Court reasoned that Title VII could not be read literally; that reasonable attempts to remedy "conspicuous racial imbalance in traditionally segregated categories" is not "race" discrimination within the broad purpose of Title VII to promote equal employment opportunity for racial minorities. *Johnson v. Transportation Agency, Santa Clara County* (S.Ct.1987) applied this reasoning to affirmative action based on gender.

Governmentally adopted affirmative action plans have been upheld, but they may have to meet the slightly higher "strict scrutiny" standards imposed by the Constitution. *United States v. Paradise* (S.Ct.1987).

## § 9.03  The Standards for Legal Affirmative Action

*a.  A Plan and Its Justification*

Race or sex discrimination against white males cannot be justified by labeling *ad hoc* racially premised decisions as "affirmative action." To justify decisions that use race, ethnic origin, or sex the decision must be made pursuant to a preexisting, formalized, and presumably written plan. Private employers can adopt affirmative action plans only in response to an identified "conspicuous racial imbalance in traditionally segregated job categories". While a finding or admission of illegal conduct, or even the existence of an arguable case of illegality, is not required, *United Steel-workers v. Weber,* supra, an employer may not undertake affirmative action based on a general desire to increase opportunities for minorities or to rectify broader societal discrimination.  Thus, a college with a predominately black faculty could not favor a black candidate over a white candidate on the grounds that other institutions discriminate against black academicians or that in society as a whole there is a dramatic underrepresentation of black professors.  See *Hammon v. Barry* (D.C.Cir. 1987).

The necessary "conspicuous imbalance" must be based on a comparison of relevant job categories of the employer to the percentage of women and minorities in the area work force *qualified* to hold those jobs.  "Snap shot" comparisons that examine only the race of the surrounding area without accounting for the percentage of persons qualified to hold the jobs do not suffice.  For example, a city will not establish the necessary "conspicuous imbalance" in the officer ranks of its police department by showing only that the percentage of minority officers is less than the percentage of minority residents.  *Cygnar v. Chicago* (7th Cir.1989).

To establish the "compelling governmental interest" necessary to sustain the use of race or ethnic distinctions under the Constitution, governmental employers must make "some showing of prior discrimination by the governmental unit involved * * *.  Societal discrimination, without more, is

too amorphous a basis for imposing a racially clas-
sified remedy."  *Wygant v. Jackson Bd. of Educ.*
(S.Ct.1986).

### b.  Content of the Plan

Even where a plan can be adopted, the plan will
not be valid unless it is "reasonable."  "Reasonableness" requires:  (1) The ultimate goal of minority employment must not exceed the percentage of
*qualified* minorities reasonably available in the
market.  (2) The plan must be temporary.  Attempts to maintain a ratio after the underrepresentation has been rectified is a forbidden "quota,"
but it is not absolutely necessary for a termination
date to be written into the plan.  (3) The plan
cannot "unduly trammel" opportunities of the
white/male majority.  In this regard a plan cannot
bar hiring white males, or reserve certain positions
for minority persons.  *Cunico v. Pueblo School
Dist. No. 60* (10th Cir.1990).  Hiring criteria, such
as experience or educational credentials, can be
ignored, but a plan is not reasonable if it directs
the hiring of minority persons who cannot perform
job duties.  An employer may not alter the results
on selection tests in order to reach a desired racial
or gender result.

Hiring ratios can be used.  Indeed, *Weber* sustained a 50% or 1–1 black/white hiring ratio.  The
legality of fixed hiring ratios by governmental employers is less clear.  *Regents of University of Cal.
v. Bakke* (S.Ct.1978) (quota for college admission

unconstitutional). As an alternative to a ratio, plans may provide that decision-makers should consider race or sex a "plus" factor in selecting between qualified applicants, with the decision-maker being evaluated by superiors on the progress toward reaching the defined numerical goal. *Johnson v. Transportation Agency, Santa Clara County* (S.Ct.1987). A plan unduly trammels the interests of white workers if it requires the discharge of white employees or, if in the time of economic reversal, it permits layoffs to be allocated on racially premised ratios. *Britton v. South Bend Community School Corp.* (7th Cir.1987).

### c. The Burdens

Affirmative action is not a true defense. The employer can respond to a charge of illegal "reverse" discrimination by presenting an affirmative action plan and demonstrating that the challenged decision was made pursuant to that plan. This shifts the burden to the plaintiff to prove that the plan does not meet the standards set forth in *Weber* and *Johnson*. *Johnson v. Transportation Agency, Santa Clara County* (S.Ct.1987).

## § 9.04 Collective Bargaining Agreements and Consent Decrees

Even if lawful, and even if adopted in settlement of pending litigation, affirmative action plans unilaterally adopted by the employer do not override rights created by collective bargaining agreements.

An affirmative action plan adopted in settlement of litigation in which the employer awarded promotions according to a racially premised ratio was no defense to an action by white employees to enforce their seniority rights under a collective agreement. *W.R. Grace and Co. v. Local Union 759* (S.Ct.1983). Prior to 1992 an affirmative action plan adopted pursuant to a decree could be challenged by employees who were not parties to the suit and assert that the affirmative action plan violated their statutory or constitutional rights. *Martin v. Wilks* (S.Ct.1989). The 1991 Civil Rights Act, however, limits post-litigation challenges to persons who had no notice of the proposed order, lacked reasonable opportunity to object, and whose interests were not represented by another who had previously challenged the order on the same legal ground.

## § 9.05  Affirmative Action for Indians

"Any business or enterprise on or near an Indian reservation with respect to any publicly announced employment practice of such business or enterprise [may give] preferential treatment * * * to any individual because he is an Indian living on or near a reservation." 42 U.S.C.A. § 2000e–2(i).

# CHAPTER 10

# ILLEGALLY MOTIVATED DECISION–MAKING

## § 10.01 Introduction: A Problem of Proof

Employment discrimination law only prohibits treatment "because of" proscribed classifications. If the defendant does not admit that it used proscribed criteria, plaintiff can prevail by convincing the fact finder that the defendant's actions were actually motivated by a factor prohibited by the statutes.

## § 10.02 Motivation Proved by Direct Evidence and the Problem of "Mixed Motives"

### a. Direct Evidence

Direct evidence of illegal motive consists of spoken or written words of animus against a protected class, such as "No woman should be named to a B schedule job," *Burns v. Gadsden State Community College* (11th Cir.1990), or "If this were my company I wouldn't hire any blacks." *EEOC v. Alton Packaging Corp.* (11th Cir.1990). When such evidence is presented and challenged, it is necessary for the fact finder to resolve whether the alleged expressions were made. Plaintiff must then show

67

a link between the expressed animus and the challenged decision. This is accomplished where the statement occurs simultaneous with, or logically is related to, the challenged decision. *EEOC v. M.D. Pneumatics, Inc.* (8th Cir.1985). For example, the employer may have expressed in general terms that "women are not good sailors." Thereafter, a woman is denied, without comment, a position that requires work on a ship. Because the expression of prejudice has a logical connection to the employer's subsequent decisions, it is appropriate to infer that the prejudice influenced the decision. *Grant v. Hazelett Strip–Casting Corp.* (2d Cir.1989).

If an employer regularly makes general racial insults, such as referring to black employees as "his niggers," or labeling Mexican employees as "wet backs," it is permissible to infer that the prejudice against the slandered class influenced employment decisions. At some point, however, isolated insults, expressions of stereotyped notions, or "stray remarks" will not be sufficiently related to the decisional process to support an inference that subsequent decisions were illegally motivated. *Price Waterhouse v. Hopkins* (S.Ct.1989); *Powell v. Missouri State Highway and Transp. Dept.* (8th Cir.1987).

b.  *Mixed Motives and the "Same Decision" Defense*

A defendant may allege that notwithstanding illegal animus, it also relied on legitimate reasons for its treatment of the plaintiff. *Price Waterhouse v. Hopkins* (S.Ct.1989), held that once a plaintiff proves that illegal factors "played a motivating part in an employment decision, the defendant may avoid a finding of liability only by proving by a preponderance of the evidence that it would have made the same decision even had it not taken the plaintiff's [protected class] into account." Thus, where plaintiff proved that sexual stereotyping played a role in her rejection and defendant presented evidence that it also relied upon plaintiff's personality problems with co-workers, to avoid liability defendant must prove that it would have rejected the plaintiff based solely upon her personality problems. If it carried this burden, defendant was not liable, notwithstanding the fact that illegal motivation in fact played a role in the treatment of plaintiff. As plaintiff was not a "prevailing party" plaintiff could secure no remedy such as injunctive relief against future illegal conduct or an award of attorneys' fees.

*Price Waterhouse* prompted a provision in the Civil Rights Act of 1991. Liability attaches upon a finding that defendant utilized illegal factors in making the decision. This finding permits plaintiff to secure injunctive relief and an award of attorneys' fees even if defendant would have made the same decision for legitimate reasons.

"Mixed motive" analysis requires *simultaneous* presence of legitimate and illegitimate motivation. If legitimate grounds asserted for rejecting the plaintiff *did not exist* in the mind of the decision-maker *at the time of the decision,* defendant was motivated solely by illegal considerations and cannot avoid full remedies by asserting a hypothetical possibility that legitimate factors might have resulted in the same decision. *Sabree v. United Broth. of Carpenters & Joiners Local No. 33* (1st Cir.1990).

## § 10.03 Motivation Proved by Disparate Treatment: *McDonnell Douglas Corp. v. Green*

a. *The Three Step Minuet: An Overview of Respective Burdens*

In the absence of direct evidence, illegal motive can be established through circumstantial evidence that invokes a three step model of proof. There is no rigid formula for the first step, but generally stated, a plaintiff creates an initial inference of illegal motivation by proof that as a member of a protected class she was treated differently than a similarly situated person of another class. If plaintiff establishes such disparate treatment, step two shifts a burden to defendant to "articulate a legitimate, nondiscriminatory reason" for the treatment. *McDonnell Douglas Corp. v. Green* (S.Ct.1973). Defendant's burden is not one of persuasion; it is to produce evidence from which lawful motivation *could be* inferred. *Texas Dept. of Community Affairs v. Burdine* (S.Ct.1981). If defendant fails to present a "legitimate, nondiscriminatory" reason, judgment must be rendered for the plaintiff.

When defendant presents a legitimate, nondiscriminatory reason for its action, the inquiry moves to step three and reshifts to the plaintiff the burden to present evidence of the pretextual nature of defendant's articulated reason. "[Plaintiff] may succeed in this either directly by persuading the court that a discriminatory reason more likely motivated the employer or indirectly by showing that the employer's proffered explanation is unworthy of credence." *Texas Dept. of Community Affairs v. Burdine,* supra. If plaintiff produces no additional evidence, defendant is entitled to judgment. However, if plaintiff comes forward with sufficient evidence to raise an issue of fact as to defendant's motivation, this evidence brings into focus the ultimate factual issue. On the ultimate issue of defendant's motivation plaintiff carries the burden of persuading the fact finder by a preponderance of the evidence that defendant was illegally motivated.

The trial court's resolution of the issue of defendant's motive is a factual finding reviewed on appeal under the "clearly erroneous" standard of Rule 52(a), Fed.R.Civ.Proc. *Anderson v. Bessemer City* (S.Ct.1985). The judicially created elements for each step of the process is a common and helpful way to address this issue, but this process is not rigid, mechanized, or ritualistic. If the fact finder considers all the evidence and makes a finding on the issue of motive that correctly places the ultimate burden of persuasion on the plaintiff, if not "clearly erroneous" that finding will be affirmed on appeal, regardless of whether the trial court correctly articulated the elements of a prima facie case or identified the points where the intermediate evidentiary burdens shift between the parties. *United States Postal Service Bd. of Governors v. Aikens* (S.Ct.1983).

## b. Step One, The Prima Facie Case

*(1) Hiring and Promotion.* In hiring and promotion cases plaintiff creates an initial inference of illegal motivation by establishing five elements: (i) plaintiff was within a class protected by the statutes; (ii) plaintiff applied; (iii) defendant had a vacancy for which it was seeking applicants; (iv) plaintiff was qualified; (v) plaintiff was denied the position and the employer continued to seek applicants or filled the position with a person from a different class. *McDonnell Douglas Corp. v. Green,* supra.

(i) "Protected Class". Generally, a plaintiff proves membership in a racial or ethnic minority, that she is female, or is over age 40. White males can create an inference of race or sex discrimination by presenting "special circumstances" that would give rise to an inference of illegal discrimination. "Special circumstances" could consist of clear disparate treatment, the decision-maker being black, or evidence of an ill defined "affirmative action" goal. *Bishopp v. District of Columbia* (D.C.Cir.1986).

(ii) "Application". Generally, if plaintiff does not apply there can be no inference of improper motivation when another person is selected. General inquiries are not an "application." *Wanger v. G.A. Gray Co.* (6th Cir.1989). However, no formal application is needed if plaintiff had no knowledge of the vacancy and defendant was aware of plaintiff's general interest in the position. *Chambers v. Wynne School Dist.* (8th Cir.1990).

(iii) "Vacancy" means that there was a job opening for which defendant was seeking applicants. Plaintiff must prove this vacancy, which can be done through proof of job postings, advertisements, or defendant's interviewing of applicants.

(iv) "Qualified". No inference of illegal motive can be inferred unless plaintiff proves that she was "qualified" for the job. She must prove that she possesses the posted credentials for the position, or if none are announced, that she has the skill, training, or ability to perform essential job duties. *Mitchell v. Baldrige* (D.C.Cir.1985). Failure of plaintiff to make a passing score on a test establishes plaintiff's lack of "qualifications." *United Ass'n of Black Landscapers v. Milwaukee* (7th Cir. 1990). Plaintiff need not prove that she was the *most qualified* applicant. If the person who received the job was more qualified than plaintiff, this can be articulated by the employer as a "legitimate, nondiscriminatory reason" for its decision, but "superior qualifications" need not be proved by plaintiff as part of a prima facie showing. *Patterson v. McLean Credit Union* (S.Ct.1989).

(v) "Plaintiff rejected, another selected". An inference of illegal motive requires proof that the employer either continued to seek other persons after the plaintiff's application was rejected, or simultaneous with the rejection of the plaintiff, the employer selected a person of another class. Selection of another applicant of the same class as the plaintiff simultaneous with the rejection of the plaintiff effectively prohibits an inference that class membership motivated the decision. *Jones v. Western Geophysical Co.* (5th Cir.1982).

That the decision-maker is of the same class as the plaintiff does not undermine the inference of illegal motivation. *Hill v. Mississippi State Employment Service* (5th Cir.1990).

*(2) Discharge and Discipline Cases.* Generally, in discharge cases a prima facie case of discrimination is established if plaintiff proves that she is a member of a protected class and was discharged while a person outside the class with equal or less qualifications was hired into her position or retained in a similar job. *Perryman v. Johnson Products Co., Inc.* (11th Cir.1983). If plaintiff was replaced by another person, plaintiff must prove that she was performing at a level of the employer's legitimate expectations at the time of the discharge. Otherwise, plaintiff has not proved that she was "qualified" to continue in defendant's employment. *Ang v. Procter & Gamble Co.* (6th Cir. 1991).

If a plaintiff alleges discriminatory discipline, some courts require plaintiff to isolate a person of a different class who engaged in similar conduct and who was not treated with similar harshness. *Moore v. Charlotte* (4th Cir.1985). If the plaintiff loses work by virtue of major layoffs or reorganization some courts require direct, circumstantial, or statistical evidence that a forbidden classification was utilized. The mass layoff is itself a legitimate reason for the treatment of plaintiff unless plaintiff has evidence suggesting discrimination in the way layoffs were distributed. *Johnson v. Minnesota Historical Soc.* (8th Cir.1991).

### c.  Step Two, Defendant's Burden

Once plaintiff establishes a prima facie case, defendant must articulate, through the presentation of admissible evidence, *a reason* for its treatment of the plaintiff, and must introduce evidence that it actually utilized the reason in making its decision. Allegations in the pleadings, argument of counsel, speculation by the trial court as to possible reasons, or testimonial assertions of good faith by defendant will not suffice. *Texas Dept. of Community Affairs v. Burdine* (S.Ct.1981).

Defendant's burden is not onerous, but the reason presented must be "legitimate", "nondiscriminatory", "clear and reasonably specific." It must be of sufficient rationality to permit a fact finder to infer that the reason, rather than illegitimate concerns, motivated the employer's action. Thus, a reason is legitimate even though it is not manifestly related to safe and efficient operations. *McDonnell Douglas Corp. v. Green* (S.Ct.1973). A reason is not "discriminatory" because its use has an adverse effect on a protected class, and it is not deprived of legitimacy simply because the employer could have used an alternative that would have had less of an effect on plaintiff's class. *Furnco Const. Corp. v. Waters* (S.Ct.1978). By contrast, reasons which are anti-social, illegal, or totally idiosyncratic are not legitimate because they cannot support an inference of lawful motivation. *In re Lewis* (6th Cir.1988). *Cf. Hill v. Mississippi State Employ. Service* (5th Cir.1990) (employer's incompetence and inefficiency is legitimate reason for plaintiff's rejection).

A wide range of reasons meet the standard of being "legitimate" including, "[s]eniority, length of service in the same position, personal characteristics, general education, technical training, experience in comparable work, or any combination of them." *IMPACT v. Firestone* (11th Cir.1990). Past misconduct, *McDonnell Douglas Corp. v. Green,* supra, preferring known applicants, rather than unknown "walk-on" candidates, *Furnco Const. Corp. v. Waters,* supra, and personality conflicts, *Texas Dept. of Community Affairs v. Burdine* supra, likewise have been sustained as "legitimate" reasons for making a decision.

Vague or subjective reasons, because they may mask prejudice and cannot be effectively challenged, often lack legitimacy. Subjectivity is legitimate when used to fill management or professional positions, but illegitimate where qualifications can be objectively measured or when it is used to justify selection of a person who failed to meet minimum objective standards. Compare, *Farber v. Massillon Bd. of Educ.* (6th Cir.1990) with *Lucas v. Burnley* (4th Cir.1989).

### d.  Step Three, "Pretext": Plaintiff's Burden of Persuasion

Once defendant presents evidence of a reason that is "legitimate" and "non-discriminatory," the burden reshifts to plaintiff to carry the ultimate burden of persuading the fact finder of defendant's illegal motive. This evidence can take many forms. Superior qualifications and high performance evaluations of the plaintiff compared to the minimal qualifications of his replacement support a finding of illegal motivation. *Norris v. Hartmarx Specialty Stores, Inc.* (5th Cir.1990). Statistical underrepresentation of plaintiff's class, racist/sexist insults, *Peters v. Jefferson Chemical Co.* (5th Cir. 1975), failure of the employer to rely on the reason in past decision-making, *Corley v. Jackson Police Dept.* (5th Cir.1978), failure of defendant to articulate the reason at the time of discharge and advancing conflicting reasons as the litigation progressed, *Lindahl v. Air France* (9th Cir.1991), and the presence of alternative selection devices that better served the employer's purposes without having the same discriminatory effect, *Furnco Const. Corp. v. Waters,* supra, all suggest improper motivation or the pretextual nature of defendant's articulated reason.

The general credibility of the witnesses articulating the reasons can be explored. Inconsistencies and conflicts in the testimony of defendant's decision-makers suggest the pretextual nature of any single reason. *Tye v. Board of Educ. of Polaris Joint Vocational School Dist.* (6th Cir.1987). The courts are divided on whether a finding that the articulated reason is a pretext is sufficient, without additional or direct evidence of defendant's illegal motivation, to support a judgment for the plaintiff. Compare *Patchell v. Red Apple Enterprises, Ltd.* (8th Cir.1990) with *Spencer v. General Electric Co.* (4th Cir.1990).

## § 10.04  Improperly Motivated Identical Treatment

Disparate treatment is a vehicle to establish illegal motivation; it is not necessary to establish liability. If the action of the employer is motivated by the race, gender, national origin, religion, age, or disability of the employees, its action is illegal even if all persons within the job classification are treated the same. To illustrate, a demanding weight and personal grooming obligation imposed on an all-female work force *because the work force is female* is illegal sex discrimination. *Gerdom v. Continental Airlines, Inc.* (9th Cir.1982).

Uniform use of an objective test is race discrimination if the test was adopted for the purpose of reducing the number of minority employees. *Albemarle Paper Co. v. Moody* (S.Ct.1975).

## § 10.05   Systemic Discrimination: A Pattern of Illegal Motivation

### a.   *The Teamsters Model: Respective Burdens*

Motive can be proved through statistics. *International Broth. of Teamsters v. United States* (S.Ct. 1977) provides the model. The plaintiff in *Teamsters* demonstrated that in some geographical areas where blacks constituted over 30% of the population, the employer had virtually no minority workers. In the more desirable job of "line driver" 0.4% were black and 0.3% were Hispanic. Relying on the Title VII proviso which prohibits "preferential treatment" based "solely" on a racial imbalance (42 U.S.C.A. § 2000e–2(j)), defendant argued that such comparative data could not establish Title VII liability. The Court held, however, that judicial reliance on comparative data did not require an employer "to grant preferential treatment." The data was not the basis for liability, but merely provided evidence of illegal motivation. Moreover, because plaintiff presented specific examples of disparate treatment of minority workers, liability was not premised "solely" on the basis of a racial imbalance.

*Teamsters* concluded that the virtual absence of minority workers, when unexplained, is sufficient

to establish a pattern of illegally motivated decision-making. The employer could refute such a
demonstration by showing that plaintiff's statistics
were inaccurate or insignificant or by providing a
non-discriminatory explanation for the apparently
discriminatory result, but assertions of good faith
or hiring only the most qualified applicants will
not refute a statistical showing of systemic discrimination.

If defendant fails to refute plaintiff's statistical
showing, plaintiff's evidence of systemic motivation
creates an inference that each hiring decision was
infected by illegal motivation. At this point the
litigation progresses to the remedy stage. To secure a personal remedy for an individual claimant,
plaintiff must prove that the claimant applied for a
position and was rejected *or* was deterred from
applying because of the defendant's discriminatory
practices. *Teamsters,* supra.

Once plaintiff establishes "applicant" status for
a claimant, the burden shifts to defendant. Defendant may avoid individual liability as to that
claimant only by proving that the "applicant" was
not hired for legitimate reasons, such as lack of a
vacancy or the superior qualifications of the person
selected. Defendant's burden is one of proving
that legitimate reasons actually motivated the applicant's rejection. *Teamsters,* supra.

## b.  *Problems of Statistical Proof:  Hazelwood*

*Hazelwood School Dist. v. United States* (S.Ct. 1977) specifically sanctioned the use of mathematical doctrines of statistical analysis to create the inference of systemic motivation.  In particular the Court relied upon the concept known as the "rule of exclusion" or standard deviation analysis.

Standard deviation analysis has three steps.  It involves: (1) identifying the expected number, or value;  (2) determining the difference between the expected number and the number actually observed;  and (3) applying a mathematical formula to that difference which calculates the probabilities that the difference between the expected number and the observed number was a product of chance.

The observed number is the employer's actual experience, for example, the percentage of minority workers in the employer's work force or the percentage of women and minority applicants hired during a particular period.  In *Hazelwood,* one observed number was that in two years 1.4% and 1.8% of the total number of teachers working for defendant were black.  Another observed number was that 3.7% of the recently hired teachers were black.

The expected number is a determination of a percentage of employees by race or sex that one would anticipate if random choice were in operation.  In an employment context this often requires first identifying the geographical area from which the employer would draw workers.  In *Ha-*

*zelwood,* since 5.7% of the teachers in the county where the Hazelwood school was located were black, *if* the school selected its teachers from the county, one would expect a random selection to result in 5.7% of the school's teachers being black. However, *if* defendant recruited from the entire metropolitan area (city and county), where 15.4% of teachers were black, the expected percentage of black teachers produced by a random selection would be 15.4%. The *Hazelwood* Court remanded the case to the trial court to determine, among other things, which geographical area should be used to determine the expected value.

In determining the geographical area from which the employer would draw workers, courts regularly rely upon data in the Standard Metropolitan Statistical Area (SMSA), a demographic compilation by the United States Department of Commerce. But courts may look to recruiting patterns, unique commuting difficulties, or special affirmative action efforts to determine more precisely from where an employer would be expected to draw workers.

An expected value must determine the extent to which the qualifications of persons in that geographical area match the qualifications required by the employer. If an employer is filling jobs where the skill "involved is one that many persons possess or can readily acquire" one would expect, as for truck drivers in *Teamsters,* that the employer's work force would mirror the general, unrefined racial, ethnic, and gender composition of the area. However, if the job requires special training or skill, such as a college degree or professional certification, as in *Hazelwood* for school teachers, the expectation is that the employer's work force would have the same racial, ethnic, and gender composition as those in the area *who possess the required qualifications.*

The final step of standard deviation analysis is to answer the question whether the observed results can be explained in terms of a random selection. Standard deviation formulae provide a mathematical response to that question in terms of probabilities. As the observed outcome moves to either side of the expected outcome, the probability that the deviation was a product of chance diminishes. At some point, the statistician can conclude that the outcome is so remote from the expected value that chance is eliminated as an hypothesis.

Placed in the employment context, if an employer filled 100 unskilled vacancies and drew applicants from a pool of workers that is 50% black and 50% white, the expected value would be a work force of 50 white workers and 50 black workers. If the employer hired 48 black workers, although deviating from the expected value of 50, random selection is a viable explanation for the outcome, and thus no inference of racial discrimination can be drawn. If, however, only 15 blacks were selected, the standard deviation formula would demonstrate that such an outcome would happen so rarely that chance cannot be relied upon to explain the result. Statisticians and courts agree that if a result could be the product of chance only one time in 100 (or have a 0.01 confidence level), chance cannot be relied on as an hypothesis to explain the result. The confidence level of 0.01 is reached at 2.57 standard deviations. (For more detail with formulae see Player, Employment Discrimination Law (hornbook) pp. 343–356).

If the data eliminates chance as an explanation for the observed underrepresentation, defendant can prevail only if it presents a legitimate explanation for the result, such as establishing to the court's satisfaction that the underrepresented race or sex had no interest in, was not "qualified" for, or did not seek the jobs in question. *EEOC v. Sears, Roebuck & Co.* (7th Cir.1988).

Parties often present conflicting statistical models. The plaintiff in *Hazelwood,* for example, presented a simple "snapshot" of the employer's work force (1.8% black) and compared this to the racial composition of qualified workers in the relevant geographical area, which in *Hazelwood* was either 5.7% or 15.4% depending on whether the employer could be expected to recruit from the county or the broader metropolitan area. Defendant countered by presenting recent "applicant flow" data which demonstrated that 3.7% of the recently hired applicants were black, and argued that *if* 5.7% (the percentage of black teachers in the county) is the expected value, the difference between the observed (3.7%) and the expected (5.7%) could be a product of chance. An issue remanded to the trial court for resolution was which of the statistical models was more accurate.

Recent hiring or applicant flow data tends to be more reliable than static "snapshot" work force comparisons. Applicant flow data focuses on current decision-making; work force comparisons include persons hired in past years, and thus may tell little of the motive behind the employer's current hiring practices. However, if an employer's practices have discouraged minority persons from applying, or, conversely, if affirmative action efforts have produced disproportionately high numbers of marginally qualified minority applicants, inferences based on hiring rates are unreliable.

## § 10.06   Perpetuation of Past Segregation

Certain distinctions, neutral on their face and neutral in terms of the motivation, may perpetuate invidiously motivated distinctions. For example, prior to the effective date of Title VII, an employer paid a discriminatory wage rate to black employees and continued to use that wage as a basis for determining annual salary increases. The result was that black employees, because of prior intentional discrimination, continued to make less than similarly situated white employees. *Bazemore v. Friday* (S.Ct.1986). An employer which segregated black workers into the undesirable work units ceases discriminatory job assignments, but prohibits transfers from one unit to the other. Regardless of current motive for the no-transfer rule, its implementation perpetuates the prior segregation by freezing the victims of that segregation in the undesirable jobs. *Jones v. Lee Way Motor Freight, Inc.* (10th Cir.1970). Certain trades traditionally were limited to whites with relatives of current members being preferred. When the "whites only" rule is abolished, the preference given to relatives of current members, who necessarily are white, perpetuates the prior "whites only" rule. *Local 53, Asbestos Workers v. Vogler* (5th Cir.1969). Similarly, when an employer with a work force predominately of one race fills vacancies with friends and relatives of its employees, this nepotism perpetuates the existing racial pattern. *Thomas v. Washington County School Bd.* (4th Cir. 1990).

Once plaintiff proves the perpetuation of prior discrimination on current workers, the employer must establish the "business necessity" of the practice. In this context "business necessity" has four elements: (1) a significant business purpose; (2) that is sufficiently compelling to override any racial impact; (3) the challenged practice effectively carries out that business purpose; and (4) no acceptable alternative policies would better accomplish the business purposes. *Green v. Missouri Pac. R. Co.* (8th Cir.1975).

Business necessity cannot justify continuation of a system that perpetuates discriminatorily motivated pay rates; economic cost of equalizing wages is not a "necessity." *Bazemore v. Friday* (S.Ct. 1986). Prohibiting transfers between units, while rational in terms of predictability, efficiency, and worker morale, it is not "necessary" to insure job performance. *Jones v. Lee Way Motor Freight, Inc.* (10th Cir.1970). Preference for relatives is socially rational, but not "necessary." *Bonilla v. Oakland Scavenger Co.* (9th Cir.1982).

# CHAPTER 11

# ADVERSE IMPACT: LIABILITY IN THE ABSENCE OF MOTIVE

## § 11.01 Introduction: Griggs v. Duke Power Co.

Liability is established by proof that a selection device has an unjustified adverse impact on the employment opportunities of a class protected by the statutes. *Griggs v. Duke Power Co.* (S.Ct.1971). In *Griggs* the employer required a high school diploma and a passing score on two professionally developed tests. The lower courts concluded that Title VII requires proof of discriminatory motive, which plaintiffs failed to establish, but the Supreme Court reversed stating:

> The Act proscribes not only overt discrimination but also practices that are fair in form, but discriminatory in operation. "[A]bsence of discriminatory intent does not redeem employment procedures or testing mechanisms that operate as 'built in headwinds' for minority groups and are unrelated to measuring job capability."

Impact analysis has been applied under the ADEA, *Geller v. Markham* (2d Cir.1980), and the Rehabilitation Act. *Stutts v. Freeman* (11th Cir.

1983).  The Americans With Disabilities Act statutorily adopts, with considerable specificity, impact analysis.

## § 11.02  Plaintiff's Case: Proving Impact

*a.  Generally: The Need for Precise Proof*

Plaintiff's burden is to prove that an employment practice used by the defendant adversely affects employment opportunities of a class protected by the statute.  This burden is not carried by assumptions; plaintiff must present specific proof of impact.  For example, it cannot be assumed that traditional requirements for academic promotion adversely affect a particular race.  *Carpenter v. Board of Regents of University of Wis. System* (7th Cir.1984).

Impact is not proved by a demonstration that the employer's work force does not reflect the racial, ethnic, or gender percentages of the area's population.  An imbalanced work force may be the product of legitimate factors, such as geography, cultural differences, or the lack of unchallenged qualifications for the jobs.  Consequently, to prove impact plaintiff must show that the imbalance is "because of" the challenged device.  This requires identification of a particular device and a statistical demonstration through either "applicant flow" or "applicant pool" data of the effect that device has on the employment opportunities of a protected class.  *Wards Cove Packing Co. v. Atonio* (S.Ct.1989).

### b.  *Applicant Flow*

Applicant flow data demonstrates the impact of a device by showing significant differential selection rates between members of different classes who apply for jobs and are selected through the employer's use of the challenged device. For example, the challenged device is an objective test which the employer gives to 150 applicants, 100 of whom are white and 50 of whom are black. Seventy-five of the white applicants pass the test and twenty-five of the black applicants pass. The "applicant flow" selection rate on the test for white applicants is 75% (75 of 100); the selection rate for black applicants is 50% (25 of 50).

Plaintiff must prove that any observed difference in selection rates is significant. The EEOC considers a device to have a significant adverse impact if it produces "[a] selection rate for any race, sex, or ethnic group * * * less than four-fifths ($\frac{4}{5}$) of the rate for the group with the highest rate * * *." 29 CFR § 1607.3D. If 75% of the white applicants passed the employer's test, a four-fifths selection rate of whites is 60% (75% × $\frac{4}{5}$ = 60%). Consequently, if more than 60% of black applicants passed the test it would not have an adverse impact on black applicants. If less than 60% of the black applicants passed, the device would have an adverse impact.

An alternative to the "rule of $\frac{4}{5}$ths" is to apply standard deviation analysis to the observed applicant flow data. Supra, § 10.05(b). This statistical

technique determines whether the difference between the observed selection rates and an expected
outcome of equal selection rates could be attributed
to chance or random selection.   If chance is eliminated as an hypothesis for the lower passing rates
of one class, it is permissible to assume that the
device is adversely affecting employment opportunities of that class.   *Hameed v. International Ass'n
of Bridge, Structural and Ornamental Iron Workers*
(8th Cir.1980).

The point of measuring applicant flow must be
established.   *Connecticut v. Teal* (S.Ct.1982) involved a multi-tiered series of selection devices.
Each applicant was first given an objective screening test.   Those who failed to make a minimum
score were eliminated from further consideration.
Those who passed were evaluated using additional
criteria.   Eighty percent of the white applicants
and 54% of the black applicants passed this first
screening test, producing a selection rate for black
applicants at this point of less than $^4/_5$ of the
selection rate of white applicants.   However, the
black applicants who survived the first test were
selected using the additional criteria at a much
higher rate than the white survivors, producing a
"bottom line" selection rate of 22.9% of the initial
black applicants and 13.5% of the initial white
applicants.   Defendant argued that since the "bottom line" was that black applicants actually were
being hired at a higher rate than white applicants,
the selection *system* did not adversely affect employment opportunities of blacks.   The Court held,

however, that the focus must be upon the initial screening test which disproportionately eliminated black applicants from further consideration.

*Teal* suggests that each component of a multi-criteria system can be analyzed for its impact. Lower courts, however, limit *Teal* to the "vertical" layering of tests, in which the challenged component disqualifies applicants from further consideration. If a component is not disqualifying, as where a "horizontal" battery of tests is given with a total score calculated on the entire battery, individual scores on components are not isolated and analyzed for their discrete effect. *Sengupta v. Morrison–Knudsen Co.* (9th Cir.1986).

Applicant flow data must include sufficient numbers to make the outcome statistically significant. When a small increase in the numbers would produce radically different selection rates, the data is insufficient to prove impact. *Yartzoff v. Oregon* (9th Cir.1984). Moreover, the data must have a precise connection to the challenged device. In *New York City Transit Authority v. Beazer* (S.Ct. 1979), for example, plaintiffs challenged a rule that denied employment to persons enrolled in methadone based drug rehabilitation programs. According to plaintiff's data, 81% of all employees referred to the employer's medical director for *drug abuse* were black or Hispanic. This data was inadequate because the rule being challenged was the disqualification of persons *enrolled in drug rehabil-*

*itation programs,* not persons *referred for drug abuse.*

Applicant flow data is an unreliable measure of the impact of a credential which has a self-selecting effect on potential applicants.  For example, if an employer has an announced policy of requiring a height of 5′–8″, analyzing its effect on actual applicants would be meaningless because only those of the required height would bother to apply. *Dothard v. Rawlinson* (S.Ct.1977).  Applicant flow data is unreliable also where an employer has encouraged an artificially high number of marginally qualified persons to enter the process through affirmative action recruiting.   29 CFR § 1607.4D

c.  *"Applicant Pool"*

"Applicant pool" proof analyzes whether persons from different classes within the *potential* applicant pool possess a challenged credential at rates which differ along class lines.  There is no examination of the employer's actual experience.  The impact of a rule or credential is determined by comparing the percentages of minority to non-minority persons who live in the area from which an employer draws its work force and who possess the challenged credential.

Applicant pool data requires plaintiff to identify the geographic area from which an employer would be expected to draw workers.  For example, the impact of a high school diploma requirement was established in *Griggs v. Duke Power Co.* (S.Ct.1971) by census data showing that in the State of North Carolina (the "applicant pool" from which the employer was assumed to have drawn workers), 34% of the white males had high school diplomas compared to only 12% of the black males in the State. Plaintiff in *Dothard v. Rawlinson,* supra, demonstrated the adverse impact on women of a height and weight requirement for Alabama prison guards by proof from statistical abstracts that 99% of the men in the United States would meet the requirement but only 59% of the women would qualify. *Dothard* relied on national height and weight data, rather than state data, under the reasonable assumption that such data would remain constant throughout the nation.

To be a reliable indicia of the impact of a particular credential, the applicant pool also must be refined to account for persons who, aside from the challenged credential, would be unqualified or uninterested in the position. *New York City Transit Authority v. Beazer* (S.Ct.1979) addressed the impact of a practice of refusing to employ persons in drug rehabilitation programs. The area's population was 36% minority, but 63% of the persons in the area's public rehabilitation programs were minorities. The Court rejected this data as proof of impact in part because many persons in such rehabilitation programs might be otherwise disqualified because they lacked unchallenged job qualifications such as educational minima or the absence of a criminal record.

## § 11.03　Justifying Impact: Defendant's Burden

If plaintiff proves the impact of a device on a protected class, the burden shifts to the defendant to justify its use of the challenged device. *Griggs* characterized this burden as "business necessity," but suggested that exclusionary practices would be justified if "manifestly related" to job duties. Between 1971, when *Griggs* was decided, and 1989 the courts used "business necessity" and "manifestly related" interchangeably. The courts agreed, however, that the burden of proving "business necessity" was upon the defendant.

*Wards Cove Packing Co. v. Atonio* (S.Ct.1989) diluted the concept of "business necessity" and realigned the burdens. Once plaintiff established that an identified device had an adverse effect on a particular class:

> [T]he dispositive issue is whether the challenged practice serves, in a significant way, the legitimate goals of the employer. * * * A mere insubstantial justification in this regard will not suffice, * * *. At the same time, though, there is no requirement that the challenged practice be 'essential' or 'indispensable' to the employer's business to pass muster.

As to defendant's burden regarding proof:

> [T]he employer carries the burden of producing evidence of a business justification for his employment practice. The burden of persuasion,

however, remains with the disparate-impact plaintiff.

Moreover, *Wards Cove* held that plaintiff's presentation of alternatives does not establish the illegitimacy of the device. Rather, alternatives suggest, but do not prove, improper motivation for use of the device.

The Civil Rights Act of 1991 overturns *Wards Cove.* The Act places the burden of persuasion back upon the employer by defining "demonstrate" to mean "meets the burdens of production and persuasion," and then making it an unlawful employment practice where plaintiff demonstrates that a particular practice causes a disparate impact on a protected class "and the respondent fails to demonstrate that the challenged practice is job related * * * and consistent with business necessity." It is also unlawful for defendant to refuse to adopt known alternatives which have a less discriminatory impact and serve equally well the employer's business purpose.

## § 11.04  Impact Analysis Applied to Subjective Decisions

*Watson v. Fort Worth Bank and Trust Co.* (S.Ct. 1988) involved a black woman employee who repeatedly had been denied promotions. The employer justified each of its decisions through subjective comparisons of the plaintiff to other candidates. The Supreme Court held that plaintiff could prevail if she could prove the ultimate impact of the subjective system on black applicants, and if, upon proof of such impact, the employer was unable to justify the "legitimacy" of its subjective process. *Wards Cove Packing Co. v. Atonio,* supra, dilutes the effect of *Watson* by holding that mere racial imbalance in the employer's work force would not prove the adverse impact of a subjective system. Plaintiff must present applicant flow data demonstrating the extent to which otherwise qualified minority applicants were disproportionately eliminated by the subjective process.

If plaintiff proves the impact of the subjective system on her class, an employer may find it difficult to establish the business necessity of subjective criteria in selecting semi-skilled jobs such as clericals, mechanics, factory workers, or truck drivers. *Rowe v. Cleveland Pneumatic Co.* (6th Cir. 1982). However, subjectivity is necessary where objective devices cannot be devised to evaluate fairly the qualities needed for successful job performance, as in the case of managers, supervisors, academics, artists, or professionals. *Lieberman v. Gant* (2d Cir.1980).

## § 11.05 Impact Analysis Applied to Non–Testing Devices

Educational credentials such as diplomas, degrees, and certificates often can be proved to adversely affect minority applicants by reference to applicant pool data demonstrating that certain groups do not possess the required credential at a rate comparable to the general population. While strict "validation" of such devices is not required, *Hawkins v. Anheuser—Busch* (8th Cir.1983), such credentials will not be assumed to be job related and necessary unless the job requires a skill directly related to the educational credential. General educational credentials, such as a high school diploma, are not necessary for selecting employees to fill lower level or semi-skilled jobs. *Griggs v. Duke Power Co.,* supra. It is legitimate, however, to require a degree in library science for the position of librarian, an accounting degree for an accountant, or even a general college degree for executives, airplane pilots, or police officers. *Walls v. Mississippi State Dept. of Public Welfare* (5th Cir.1984); *Davis v. Dallas* (5th Cir.1985).

General physical requirements such as height and weight minima rarely can be related to job requirements. *Dothard v. Rawlinson* (S.Ct.1977). However, if the job requires a particular level of strength or physical agility, testing for that ability is legitimate. For example, as the job of fire fighter requires the moving of heavy weights, it is legitimate to disqualify recruits unable to carry those weights. *Evans v. Evanston* (7th Cir.1989). Police officers can be required to demonstrate a basic level of running speed, stamina, and physical strength. *Blake v. Los Angeles* (9th Cir.1979).

The impact of disqualifying persons with criminal conviction records can be proved through statistical records showing that certain racial groups suffer higher conviction rates than society as a whole. Such a disqualification is a business necessity if the position being filled requires trust and integrity. However, if the job is such that the employer or the public is placed at little risk from any recidivist criminal behavior, for example in an outdoor maintenance job, the exclusion of those with criminal records may not be a business necessity. *Green v. Missouri Pac. R. Co.* (8th Cir.1977).

## § 11.06 Impact Analysis and Scored Tests

### a. *Generally*

Title VII has a proviso relating to testing:

[N]or shall it be an unlawful employment practice for an employer to give and to act upon the results of any professionally developed ability test provided that such test, its administration or action upon the results is not designed, intended, or used to discriminate because of race, color, religion, sex or national origin.

42 U.S.C.A. § 2000e–2(h).

In *Griggs v. Duke Power Co.* (S.Ct.1971) the employer asserted that this proviso preserved its right to use two tests because, in the words of the statute, they were "professionally developed" and were "not designed, intended, or used to discriminate." The Court found, however, that notwithstanding the employer's good faith, the tests were not saved because the testing proviso preserves only tests proved by the employer to be "job related." According to *Griggs,* a test that has an adverse impact and is not "job related," is being "used to discriminate":

What Congress has forbidden is giving these devices and mechanisms controlling force unless they are demonstrably a reasonable measure of job performance * * *. What Congress has commanded is that any tests used must measure the person for the job and not the person in the abstract.

In 1978 federal enforcement agencies promulgated the current Uniform Guidelines on Employee Selection Procedures, 29 CFR Part 1607. These guidelines require formalized validation according to standards of the American Psychological Association. *Albemarle Paper Co. v. Moody* (S.Ct.1975) held that such guidelines were entitled to great judicial deference, emphasizing that "discriminatory tests are impermissible unless shown by professionally acceptable methods, to be 'predictive of or significantly correlated with important elements of work behavior which comprise or are relevant to the job or jobs for which candidates are being evaluated.'" The Court demanded of employers detailed and precise statistical validation and directed lower courts to measure defendant's evidence against the demands of the Guidelines. The general reputation or widespread use of a test, or casual reports of its reliability, could not be accepted in lieu of documentary evidence of validity. Undocumented expert opinion does not suffice. 29 CFR § 1607.9. A test validated by one employer will be valid for use by other employers only upon proof that job duties at the two locations are the same.

The 1991 Civil Rights Act places the burden of establishing the test's validity on the defendant, but prohibits employers from adjusting test scores or using different cutoff scores on the basis of race, sex, religion, or national origin. Thus, an employer may not avoid an obligation to validate a test by adjusting the test scores of a class in a way that eliminates the adverse impact of the test on that class.

### b. Content Validity

The simplest form of test validation is where the test replicates major portions of the job, as for example, where a test measuring typing or computer literacy is used to select a secretarial support person, *Herd v. Allegheny County* (W.D.Pa.1979), or a welding test is used to select a welder. *Ligons v. Bechtel Power Corp.* (8th Cir.1980). A content valid test must measure or replicate a "representative sample" of the job's duties. It is not valid if it measures only a small portion of those duties. 29 CFR § 1607.14C(4). For example, fire fighters may need to write reports, but a grammar test is too narrow to be content valid.

Pen and paper tests lack content validity for a job that requires a particular skill or physical activity. *Firefighters Inst. for Racial Equality v. St. Louis* (8th Cir.1977). However, if the job requires specific knowledge, such as the need for teachers to know the subject matter taught or for police officers to know criminal law, pen and paper tests that measure such knowledge are valid. *United States v. South Carolina* (D.S.C.1977). Content validation cannot be used to measure general traits thought to be desirable in all persons, such as intelligence, honesty, or patience.

The test user must set the level of successful job performance. To be valid the test must identify those who reach that level. When an *absolute* standard is required, a test is not content valid if it is used to select candidates on *relative* skill or ability above the minimum required. For example, if the job requires the ability to lift 100 pounds, but no more, a test that eliminates those who cannot lift 100 pounds is content valid. But the test will be invalid if it is used to prefer applicants who can lift 125 pounds over those who can lift 110 pounds. *Evans v. Evanston* (7th Cir. 1989). Selection according to rank on test scores is permitted only where test scores can be shown to vary directly with the level of job performance. *Police Officers for Equal Rights v. Columbus* (6th Cir.1990).

### c.  *Criterion–Related Validity*

Criterion-related validity is the statistical relationship between scores on a test and the objective measures, or criteria, of job performance. The test need not have components that resemble the job. Because criterion validation depends upon a comparison of job performance and test performance, validation first requires a detailed analysis of the job components (criteria) and an objective method of measuring or evaluating those criteria. Subjective generalized evaluation by supervisors of comparative work performance will not suffice. *Albemarle Paper Co. v. Moody* (S.Ct.1975). Employees must be evaluated according to established performance criteria. To insure that test results do not corrupt the evaluation process, test scores must not be available to performance evaluators.

The job performance being evaluated must be that which the test taker would assume upon being employed or after a brief orientation period. If job progression is not automatic or there is a significant time span between initial employment and advancement, performance at a higher level job may not be used as a criterion to select entry level workers. 29 CFR § 1607.51.

Performance in training, as opposed to actual job performance, may be used as a criterion measure if the training has a content relationship to future job duties. Thus, a test was validated by comparing test scores with performance in police academy, where academy training replicated actual duties of a police officer. *Washington v. Davis* (S.Ct. 1976).

After test performance is calculated and the performance of employees' on-the-job criteria is measured, the scores are plotted to secure a practical "correlation coefficient" between test score and job performance. *Boston Chapter, N.A.A.C.P. v. Beecher* (1st Cir.1974). Absent a "practical correlation" the test is not valid. Where there is a correlation between test score and job performance, the correlation is measured for its "statistical significance." "Statistical significance" calculates the probabilities that the "practical correlation" was a product of chance. Supra, § 10.05(b). If the analysis demonstrates significance of 0.05 or lower, meaning that the positive "practical correlation" between test scores and job performance would occur by chance no more than 1 time in 20, courts will accept the hypothesis that the test predicts job performance with sufficient accuracy to be "validated." If the job requires a high level of human or economic risk, as with airline pilots, police officers, or health care providers, a significantly lower level of correlation is demanded. 29 CFR § 1607.-6B.

A validation study should include an investigation of "unfairness" or cultural bias in the test. "Unfairness" is an hypothesis, not uniformly accepted by testing experts, that a test predicting job performance of white employees may not predict performance of persons from different backgrounds or cultures. One way to insure against "unfairness" is to conduct separate or "differential validation" studies for each cultural class. Test scores

of racial minorities are compared to job performance scores of racial minorities; test scores of non-
minorities are compared to job performance scores
of non-minorities. "Practical correlation" and
"statistical significance" are calculated separately
for each racial group. If no correlation exists as to
a class, the test wil be deemed "unfair" and may
not be used to select employees who are members
of that class.

The EEOC will not require differential validation where not technically feasible, particularly
if there is no positive showing of "unfairness" in
the test and the sample used in the validation
study includes a representative cross-section of all
classes. 29 CFR § 1707.14B.

The preferred method of conducting a validation
study, and the one requiring the fewest number of
participants to provide statistical reliability, is a
predictive study. All applicants are given the test
before beginning work. All applicants, or a representative sample, are hired. After a brief orientation period, job performance of each tested employee is evaluated, and job performance is compared
to test performance.

A second method is concurrent validation. Incumbent employees are simply given the test, and
their test scores are compared to their job performance evaluations. Or, incumbent employees who
were selected on the basis of the test will have
their job performance measured and compared to
their previous test score. Concurrent validation

has a number of practical difficulties. Nonetheless, if these difficulties are identified and accounted for in the study, reliable correlations can be established.

### d. Construct Validation

Construct validation identifies a psychological trait or characteristic ("construct") which is the necessary basis for successful job performance. The test measures the presence and degree of that "construct." For example, "leadership" would be a construct for a fire captain; "patience" for a teacher. A test that accurately measured leadership would be construct valid for a fire captain; a test that measured patience would be construct valid for a teacher.

Validation of the construct requires a statistical correlation between the identified construct and job performance using standards similar to those involved in the validation of a criterion validity study. 29 CFR §§ 1607.14D(3) and (4). As a consequence, construct validation has rarely been attempted. *Black Law Enforcement Officers Ass'n v. Akron* (6th Cir.1987).

### § 11.07  Seniority: Impact and Motive

#### a.  The Seniority Proviso: Teamsters and Evans

A proviso in Title VII states:

[I]t shall not be an unlawful employment practice for an employer to apply different  * * * terms, conditions, or privileges of employment pursuant to a bona fide seniority system * * * provided that such differences are not the result of an intention to discriminate because of race, color, religion, sex, or national origin.

42 U.S.C.A. § 2000e–2(h).

This proviso was construed in *International Broth. of Teamsters v. United States* (S.Ct.1977). The employer had two employment units: intercity drivers and local drivers. By virtue of pre-Act segregation virtually all intercity drivers were white; many local drivers were racial and ethnic minorities. Through collective bargaining agreements the employer utilized competitive seniority within each unit to determine promotions and layoffs of workers in their respective units. Consequently, local drivers who had substantial local unit seniority could not use their relative seniority to bid on vacancies in the intercity unit. The Court recognized that were it not for the proviso, the seniority system would violate the Act as the system perpetuated the past segregation without evidence of "business necessity." Nonetheless, the Court concluded:

[T]he unmistakable purpose of [the seniority proviso] was to make clear that the routine application of a bona fide seniority system would not be unlawful under Title VII * * *. [T]his was the intended result even where the employer's pre-Act discrimination resulted in whites having greater existing seniority rights than negroes.

\* \* \* [A]n otherwise neutral, legitimate seniority system does not become unlawful under Title VII simply because it may perpetuate pre-Act discrimination.

*United Air Lines v. Evans* (S.Ct.1977) expanded *Teamsters* by holding that employers may utilize seniority systems that perpetuate post-Act, and thus illegal, discrimination. In *Evans* the plaintiff, a woman, was employed as an airline flight attendant. When she married, the defendant discharged her pursuant to its no-marriage rule, which the Court assumed was illegal sex discrimination. However, plaintiff did not challenge her discharge. Years later, after defendant eliminated the no-marriage rule, plaintiff was rehired. The collective bargaining agreement provided that employees lost accumulated seniority if there was a significant break in service, and thus under the agreement plaintiff could not claim the seniority that she had earned prior to her illegal discharge. Plaintiff argued that since the break in service was caused by *illegal* sex discrimination, the contract provision prohibiting her from claiming seniority was not saved by the statute's seniority proviso.

The Court refused to distinguish between pre-Act legal segregation and unchallenged post-Act illegality. The Court held that absent a timely challenge to the discharge, the illegal treatment of plaintiff had "no present legal consequences":

[A] challenge to a neutral [seniority] system may not be predicated on the mere fact that a past event which has no present legal significance has affected the calculation of seniority credit, even if the past event might at one time have justified a valid claim against the employer.

Thus, if an individual is illegally discriminated against in a job assignment and the victim files a timely charge, the court, as a remedy, will order the victim be given the job discriminatorily denied with full seniority running from the date of the illegal treatment. *Franks v. Bowman Transp. Co., Inc.* (S.Ct.1976). However, if the victim does not file a timely challenge, subsequent decisions affecting the plaintiff made pursuant to the seniority system cannot be attacked on the basis that the system perpetuates the effects of prior illegal treatment.

All bona fide systems, those adopted prior to the effective date of Title VII and those adopted thereafter, are within the protection of the proviso. *American Tobacco Co. v. Patterson* (S.Ct. 1982).

The seniority proviso does not establish a true defense but is "a provision that itself 'delineates which employment practices are illegal and therefore prohibited and which are not.'" *Lorance v. AT & T Technologies, Inc.* (S.Ct.1989). Defendant must present and establish the objective elements of the seniority system and that the decision was made pursuant to that system. Plaintiff has the burden of proving improper motivation behind defendant's adoption or use of the system.

## b. The Seniority Proviso Applied

*(1) "System": California Brewers.* To be protected under the seniority proviso, the decision must be made pursuant to an existing and formalized "system." *California Brewers Ass'n v. Bryant* (S.Ct.1980) provides a definition:

"Seniority" is a term that connotes length of employment. A "seniority system" is a scheme that, alone or in tandem with non-"seniority" criteria, allots to employees ever improving employment rights and benefits as their relative lengths of pertinent employment increases. * * * [T]he principal feature of any and every "seniority system" is that preferential treatment is dispensed on the basis of some measure of time served in employment.

If the system does not meet the above definition, the proviso will have no application and traditional impact analysis will be applied. To be protected the system need not be a product of a collective bargaining agreement, but it must be more than informal, *ad hoc* decision-making that takes into account in an imprecise way relative length of service. *Williams v. New Orleans S.S. Ass'n* (5th Cir.1982).

The system may utilize objective distinctions as a necessary adjunct to the operation of time measurement. For example, *United Air Lines v. Evans,* supra, recognized that a rule providing for a loss of seniority through a break in service was ancillary to the seniority system and protected by the proviso. *California Brewers Ass'n v. Bryant,* supra, held that a rule that required an employee to work a minimum of 45 weeks per year to be considered "permanent," and thus entitled to special benefits, was a protected adjunct of a seniority system. A proviso that grants priority to "surplus" workers currently working over employees on layoff is a protected part of a system even though some employees on layoff may have greater length of service than working "surplus" employees. *Altman v. AT & T Technologies, Inc.* (7th Cir.1989).

*California Brewers* cautioned that a system could not "depart fundamentally from commonly accepted notions concerning acceptable contours of a seniority system, simply because those rules are dubbed 'seniority' * * *." The Court indicated, for example, that an educational requirement or successful completion of a pen and paper test could not be imposed as a condition to the operation of the seniority system and be considered within the special protections of the proviso. Identifying which adjuncts to seniority are protected may be difficult. For example, a rule that does not permit the carrying of unit seniority to another unit was part of the seniority system approved in *Teamsters.* An absolute prohibition against transfers between units is not ancillary to the system, and thus is not protected by the proviso. *Hebert v. Monsanto Co.* (5th Cir.1982).

*(2) "Good Faith".* *Teamsters* held that the legitimacy of seniority systems requires not only objective rationality but subjective good faith of the
employer in adopting and implementing the system, and the Court listed four factors to support its
conclusion that the system was "bona fide": (1) It
applied equally to all persons; (2) the units were
rational in that they followed industry practice
and were consistent with Labor Board precedents;
(3) it did not have its genesis in racial discrimination; and (4) it was maintained free from any
illegal racial purpose. Trial courts, however, look
to the totality of the circumstances suggesting the
parties' motivation and do not simply tally up the
four factors mentioned in *Teamsters.* *Harvey by
Blankenbaker v. United Transp. Union* (10th Cir.
1989).

Plaintiff must prove the lack of bona fides in
defendant's adoption or application of the system.
A finding thereon is one of fact which will be set
aside on appeal only if "clearly erroneous." *Pullman–Standard v. Swint* (S.Ct.1982).

c. *Timing of the Challenge: Statute of Limitations*

In *Lorance v. AT & T Technologies* (S.Ct.1989)
the employer had in place a seniority system which
it revised in 1979. The effect of the revision was to
provide workers in job categories occupied predominately by men greater job security in relationship
to jobs occupied predominately by women. In
1982, economic adjustments resulted in a number

of women being demoted who would not have been affected had the pre–1979 seniority system remained in effect. Three women filed charges alleging invidious motivation behind the 1979 modifications. Their charges, the Court held, were untimely. Since the issue was the motive behind the adoption of the system, the time for filing a challenge began to run the day the system was adopted, in this case 1979, not in 1982 when plaintiffs first suffered the adverse consequences of defendant's action.

The Civil Rights Act of 1991 reverses *Lorance* by providing that the time to challenge the good faith of a seniority system commences with the adoption of the system, when the individual becomes subject to the system, or from the date at which the system was applied to the injury of the plaintiff.

\*

# PART III

# PROTECTED CLASSES AND APPLICATION OF BASIC CONCEPTS

## CHAPTER 12

## RACE AND COLOR

### § 12.01 "Race," "Color," and Title VII

"Race" and "color" discrimination are proscribed by Title VII. It prohibits discrimination because of a person's racial origins in Africa or Asia, as well as discrimination against indigenous Americans such as Eskimos, Native Hawaiians, and American Indians. Whites, Europeans, or Caucasians are protected against race discrimination under the same standards as racial minorities. *McDonald v. Santa Fe Trail Transp. Co.* (S.Ct.1976). Preferring a person based on the relative lightness of skin complexion is "color" discrimination. *Walker v. Secretary of Treasury, I.R.S.* (N.D.Ga.1989).

While the wording of the Act prohibits discrimination because of "such individual's race," it has been construed to prohibit discrimination because of the race of the spouse of the applicant or em-

115

ployee. *Parr v. Woodmen of the World Life Ins. Co.*
(11th Cir.1986). It is unclear whether it is race
discrimination to hire or promote a white applicant
over a black applicant based on a social or family
connection between the white supervisor and the
white applicant. Compare *Roberts v. Gadsden Memorial Hosp.* (11th Cir.1988) with *Holder v. Raleigh* (4th Cir.1989).

## § 12.02  "Race" and the 1866 Civil Rights Act
*a.  "Race" Defined*

The portion of the 1866 Civil Rights Act codified
in 42 U.S.C.A. § 1981 provides that "all persons"
shall have the same right to make and enforce
contracts "as is enjoyed by white citizens". This
broad language reaches the employment "contract," but only proscribes "racial" discrimination.
*Saint Francis College v. Al—Khazraji* (S.Ct.1987).
"Race" has been broadly defined, however, to mean
"identifiable classes of persons * * * [based on]
their ancestry or ethnic characteristics * * *."
This concept of "race" prohibits discrimination
against Iraqis and Jews because of their ethnic
origins, as opposed to their nationality or religion.
*Saint Francis College v. Al—Khazraji,* supra, and
*Shaare Tefila Congregation v. Cobb* (S.Ct.1987).
Latinos and "hyphenated-Americans" fall within
this broad definition of "race." White persons are
protected against race discrimination under the
same standards as are applied to racial minorities.

*McDonald v. Santa Fe Trail Transp. Co.* (S.Ct. 1976).

### b.  Scope of the 1866 Act

The 1866 Civil Rights Act does not reach discrimination based on sex, religion, age, or citizenship. *Bhandari v. First Nat. Bank of Commerce* (5th Cir.1987). The Act is violated only by racially motivated discrimination; a system or selection device adversely affecting a racial group does not state a § 1981 claim. The racial animus necessary for liability, however, need not connote hostility or dislike of a race, only that race was a significant factor in the decision. *General Bldg. Contractors Ass'n v. Pennsylvania* (S.Ct.1982). The models and standards of proving illegal motive developed in Title VII jurisprudence are applied to claims under § 1981. *Patterson v. McLean Credit Union* (S.Ct. 1989). See supra, Chapt. 10.

*Patterson* limited the scope of § 1981 to refusals to make and enforce contracts, not to "post formation conduct." While the Act applied to racially motivated hiring decisions and to transfers and promotions of employees where the "nature of the change in position was such that it involved the opportunity to enter a new contract with the employer," it was held not to reach racial harassment of current employees. *Patterson v. McLean Credit*

*Union,* supra.  Logically, the discharge of an employee is a refusal to contract with that employee, but the lower courts construed *Patterson* to hold that the 1866 Act did not prohibit racially motivated discharges.  *Carter v. Sedgwick County* (10th Cir.1991).

The 1991 Civil Rights Act reversed *Patterson*'s holding by defining § 1981 "to make and enforce contracts" to include "performance, modification and termination" as well as "enjoyment of all benefits, privileges, terms and conditions of the contractual relationship."  Now racial harassment, racially premised compensation, racially motivated discharges, as well as race discrimination in hiring, transfers, and promotions are within the reach of 42 U.S.C.A. § 1981.

# CHAPTER 13

# NATIONAL ORIGIN, CITIZENSHIP, ALIENAGE

## § 13.01 "National Origin" Generally

Title VII proscribes discrimination because of "national origin." "National origin" means "the country from which your forebearers came." *Espinoza v. Farah Mfg. Co., Inc.* (S.Ct.1973). Consequently, discrimination against someone because of Italian, Latino, or Polish heritage is proscribed, *Cariddi v. Kansas City Chiefs Football Club, Inc.* (8th Cir.1977), as is favoring ethnic minorities, such as Puerto Ricans, over persons of Anglo heritage. *Earnhardt v. Puerto Rico* (1st Cir.1984). "National origin" includes distinct cultural heritage or geographic origins even if no current nation exists. Thus, discrimination against Armenians, Cajuns, or Gypsies is "national origin" discrimination. *Pejic v. Hughes Helicopters* (9th Cir.1988).

Title VII specifically permits employers to refuse employment if the position or access to the premises requires the individual to have a security clearance from the federal government and the individual cannot secure the necessary clearance. 42

U.S.C.A. § 2000e–2(g). Thus, although a denial of a security clearance is based on the origins of the individual or his family, the Act specifically allows the discrimination.

The Immigration Reform and Control Act of 1986, 8 U.S.C.A. § 1324B(1)(A), in addition to proscribing "citizenship" discrimination, prohibits national origin discrimination by employers of more than three employees that are not covered by Title VII.

## § 13.02  Language Discrimination

Requiring employees *to be able* to communicate in English is not facial national origin discrimination, and thus the employer does not have to justify such a requirement as being a bona fide occupational qualification. *Frontera v. Sindell* (6th Cir. 1975). And even though a requirement of basic fluency in English adversely affects employment opportunities of those of non-Anglo origins, it is a "business necessity" for the English speaking employer to be able to communicate with employees and for employees to communicate with each other. *Vasquez v. McAllen Bag & Supply Co.* (5th Cir.1981). Moreover, it is not "national origin" discrimination to refuse to employ an individual who must meet the public or customers but who cannot converse in English at a level necessary to communicate freely during those contacts. *Fragante v. Honolulu* (9th Cir.1989).

An employer who selects between applicants based upon their *relative* facility with English will have more difficulty in demonstrating "business necessity." If the job requires a high level of English proficiency, such as is required of police officers, writers, librarians, or teachers, a test that accurately measures the relative proficiency may be justified as a "business necessity." *Washington v. Davis* (S.Ct.1976). However, if *relative* language skill has little relationship to actual job content, the test will not be "necessary."

Discrimination against those who speak English with a "foreign" *accent* is facial national origin discrimination. *Berke v. Ohio Dept. of Public Welfare* (6th Cir.1980). Unless the accent would make the applicant's job performance unsatisfactory, as might be the case for a radio announcer, it will be very difficult for an employer to establish that accentless English is a BFOQ. See *Jurado v. Eleven—Fifty Corp.* (9th Cir.1987).

## § 13.03　Alienage and Citizenship

*a.　Title VII of the 1964 Civil Rights Act*

Title VII's prohibition against national origin discrimination does not *per se* prohibit employers from hiring only United States citizens. *Espinoza v. Farah Mfg. Co., Inc.* (S.Ct.1973). An employer may not, however, make distinctions *between aliens* based on different origins of their citizenship, e.g., accepting Canadians while rejecting Mexicans.

Lower courts have assumed, however, that discrimination *against* Americans, based on their lack cf citizenship in a foreign country, is national origin discrimination. Thus, an employer violates Title VII by preferring Korean nationals over U.S. citizens. *MacNamara v. Korean Air Lines* (3d Cir. 1988). A distinction is thus drawn between discrimination against *aliens,* which is not national origin discrimination, and discrimination against U.S. *citizens,* which is.

If the preference for nationals of the foreign employer is authorized by treaty between the United States and the government of the guest employer, the treaty may supersede Title VII prohibitions against national origin discrimination. *Sumitomo Shoji America v. Avagliano* (S.Ct.1982). While treaties often authorize a preference for nationals of the guest employer, they generally do not authorize the guest employer to discriminate on the basis of sex or race.

### b. *The Immigration Reform and Control Act of 1986*

The Immigration Act, 8 U.S.C.A. § 1324B, makes it illegal for employers to hire *undocumented* aliens. However, for all employers of more than three employees the Act prohibits discrimination in the hiring, recruitment or discharge of an individual because of such individual's "citizenship status." This prohibition is applicable *only* to citizens and "intending citizens" of the United States. A person is an "intending citizen" if she is lawfully admitted into the United States and prior to filing a charge has evidenced an intent to become a citizen by filing necessary declarations with the Immigration and Naturalization Service. The person will lose "intending citizen", and thus protected, status if she does not actually apply for citizenship within six months after first becoming eligible or fails to become naturalized within two years after the date of the application and is not actively seeking citizenship. See 29 CFR Part 44 (1991).

# CHAPTER 14

# SEX, SEXUALITY, AND PREGNANCY

## § 14.01 Generally: "Sex" Defined

Title VII proscribes discrimination because of "sex." The courts construe the word "sex" narrowly to refer to gender, not to sexuality or sexual practices. *DeSantis v. Pacific Tel. & Tel. Co., Inc.* (9th Cir.1979). Thus, it is not sex discrimination to prefer persons because of sexual attractiveness, *Malarkey v. Texaco, Inc.* (S.D.N.Y.1982), or to discharge workers because of their sexual activity or sexual morality. *Thomas v. Metroflight, Inc.* (10th Cir.1987). Men are protected against sex discrimination under the same standards as apply to women. *Diaz v. Pan Am. World Airways, Inc.* (5th Cir.1971) (female gender not BFOQ for airline flight attendant).

## § 14.02 Differing Standards and Sexual Stereotyping

It is sex discrimination to demand levels of performance or standards of conduct from members of one gender that are not required of the other gender. A rule applied only to one gender is sex discrimination. *Phillips v. Martin Marietta Corp.*

(S.Ct.1971) (no-children rule applied only to women); *Sprogis v. United Air Lines, Inc.* (7th Cir.1971) (no-marriage rule applied only to women). While it is not sex discrimination to discharge all employees who engage in extra-marital sexual relationships, *Thomas v. Metroflight, Inc.* (10th Cir.1987), it is sex discrimination to discharge a female worker for having an affair while tolerating similar conduct by male employees. *Duchon v. Cajon Co.* (6th Cir.1986). It is sex discrimination to allocate benefits, including unpaid leave, health, and retirement benefits, to women on terms that differ from those allocated to men. *Los Angeles, Dept. of Water and Power v. Manhart* (S.Ct.1978).

Employers may not measure performance in terms of sexual stereotypes relating to the proper roles and behavior of the genders. *Price Waterhouse v. Hopkins* (S.Ct.1989) involved the refusal of an accounting firm to offer a partnership to a woman associate. Plaintiff was described as "macho," "overcompensated for being a woman," "a lady using foul language," and was advised to "walk more femininely, dress more femininely, wear make-up, have her hair styled, and wear jewelry" in order to improve her chances for promotion. The Court held that the employer engaged in sex discrimination when it measured plaintiff's performance against stereotyped expectations of female behavior.

## § 14.03 Pregnancy

Title VII defines "sex" to include "pregnancy, childbirth or related conditions." That definition provides further that:

[W]omen affected by pregnancy, childbirth, or related medical conditions shall be treated the same for all employment-related purposes, including receipt of benefits under fringe benefit programs, as other persons not so affected but similar in their ability or inability to work * * *. 42 U.S.C.A. § 2000e–(k).

It is thus sex discrimination to reject a woman because of her gender, because she is pregnant, or because she has secured, or refuses to secure, an abortion. Such distinctions are legal only if the employer establishes gender or non-pregnancy as a bona fide occupational qualification reasonably necessary for actual job performance. *International Union, UAW v. Johnson Controls, Inc.* (S.Ct. 1991) (protection of the fetus does not justify BFOQ precluding employment of fertile women); *Chambers v. Omaha Girls Club, Inc.* (8th Cir.1987) (non-pregnancy out of wedlock is BFOQ for counselor of young women). Supra, Chapt. 8. Moreover, pregnancy benefits must be provided to women under the same terms as health care benefits are provided for other disabilities similarly affecting the ability to work. Infra, Chapt. 20.

It is not sex discrimination to grant pregnancy leave to women for the actual term of the disability without providing similar leave to fathers, as this "benefit" for pregnant women is mandated by the Act's requirement that pregnancy leave be accorded on terms equal to that given other disabilities. *California Fed. Sav. & Loan Ass'n v. Guerra* (S.Ct. 1987).    Nonetheless, it is sex discrimination to grant *parental leave* to female employees, apart from pregnancy disability, while denying parental leave for similarly situated male employees. *Schafer v. Board of Educ., Pittsburgh* (3d Cir.1990).

## § 14.04   Marital Status and Sexual Activity

Title VII, unlike many state statutes, does not proscribe discrimination because of "marital status."    Therefore, if the rule is applied equally to men and women, under federal law an employer may refuse to employ married persons, single persons, or married co-workers.

*Denial* of employment opportunities because a person refuses to have a sexual relationship with a supervisor is a form of sex discrimination.    Infra, § 24.02.    Whether *favoring* a paramour is sex discrimination against workers of the opposite sex, or against workers of the same sex who are not favored, has divided the courts.    Compare *King v. Palmer* (D.C.Cir.1985) with *DeCintio v. Westchester County Medical Center* (2d Cir.1986).

## § 14.05   Sexuality and Homosexuality

It is not sex discrimination to discriminate against persons who are perceived to be homosexuals, *DeSantis v. Pacific Tel. & Tel. Co., Inc.,* supra, transsexuals, bisexuals, *Ulane v. Eastern Airlines, Inc.* (7th Cir.1984), or on the basis of cross-dressing or effeminacy. *DeSantis,* supra. Presumably, favoring homosexuals of one gender over homosexuals of the other would be sex discrimination.

Two states and numerous municipalities expressly prohibit discrimination on the basis of "sexual orientation," which is defined to mean heterosexuality, homosexuality, or bisexuality.

Homosexuality is not a "handicap" as defined by the Rehabilitation Act. Even disorders such as transvestism and transsexualism are not "handicaps." *Blackwell v. U.S. Dept. of Treasury* (D.C.Cir.1987). The Americans With Disabilities Act specifically excludes from the definition of protected "disabilities" homosexuality, transvestism, and transsexualism.

# CHAPTER 15

# RELIGION AND RELIGIOUS PRACTICES

## § 15.01 Generally: "Religion" Defined

Title VII prohibits discrimination because of one's "religion" unless religion is a bona fide occupational qualification. See *Pime v. Loyola University of Chicago* (7th Cir.1986) (Catholic religion BFOQ for theology professor); *Abrams v. Baylor College of Medicine* (5th Cir.1986) (absence of Judaism not BFOQ for medical assignment to Arab country). Supra, Chapt. 8. The Act does not define "religion" except to provide that religion includes "all aspects of religious observance and practice, as well as belief." 42 U.S.C.A. § 2000e–(j). The EEOC and the courts define "religion" similar to that used when constitutional issues are addressed under the First Amendment. See *Frazee v. Illinois Dept. of Employment Security* (S.Ct.1989). "Religion" includes established and organized faiths such as Baptist, Catholic, Judaism, or Islam as well as:

> moral or ethical beliefs as to what is right and wrong which are sincerely held with the strength of traditional religious views. * * * The fact that no religious group espouses such

beliefs or the fact that the religious group to which the individual professes to belong may not accept such belief will not determine whether the belief is a religious belief of the employee or prospective employee.

29 CFR § 1605.1 (1990).

Title VII protects atheists from discrimination based on the absence of religious belief, *EEOC v. Townley Engineering & Mfg. Co.* (9th Cir.1988), and against discrimination for activity that conflicts with the employer's religious belief. *Little v. Wuerl* (3d Cir.1991) (employee who remarried after divorce was discharged because of employer's disapproval of divorce).

"Religion" does not include political beliefs or activity. Thus, while an employee's strongly held views about military draft registration is protected as "religion," *American Postal Workers Union v. Postmaster General* (9th Cir.1986), membership in the Ku Klux Klan is unprotected political activity. *Bellamy v. Mason's Stores, Inc.* (W.D.Va.1973).

## § 15.02  Religious Practices

The Act states that "religion includes all aspects of religious observances and practice." 42 U.S.C.A. § 2000e–(j). The practice need not be mandated by the religion, but it will be protected if it is assumed as part of one's religious duties. Activities such as observing Holy days, teaching a Bible study class, or attending church conventions are "religious practices." *Redmond v. GAF Corp.* (7th Cir.1978). Social or secular activity, such as sporting events or picnics, may not be "religious practices" even when sponsored by a church. *Wessling v. Kroger Co.* (E.D.Mich.1982). Protected religious practices include grooming and clothing requirements of one's religious faith. *Bhatia v. Chevron U.S.A., Inc.* (9th Cir.1984).

## § 15.03  The Duty to Accommodate Religious Practices

To establish a *prima facie* case of religious discrimination based on practices, the employee must prove that the practice is "religious," is sincerely held, inform the employer of the conflict between the practice and the employee's job obligations, and be subjected to discriminatory treatment for complying with the practice. The employer must then demonstrate "that he is unable to reasonably accommodate to [the] employee's religious observance or practice without undue hardship on the conduct of the employer's business." 42 U.S.C.A. § 2000e–(j). This duty to make "reasonable accommodations" does not require the employer to prove that the more sweeping accommodations suggested by the plaintiff would constitute an undue hardship. *Ansonia Bd. of Educ. v. Philbrook* (S.Ct. 1986). For example, *Ansonia* held that *if* the various accommodations to plaintiff's requests to observe religious holidays were "reasonable accommodations" under all of the circumstances, the employer need not prove that allowing the employee to allocate paid "personal leave" to observe additional holidays constituted an "undue hardship" on the employer.

Determining the "reasonableness" of the employer's accommodation to the employee's religious practices involves a case-by-case evaluation of the facts. In *Trans World Airlines, Inc. v. Hardison* (S.Ct.1977) the employer operated on a seven day, twenty-four hour schedule. Plaintiff's religion required observance of a Saturday Sabbath. The employee's lack of seniority, however, imposed on him a contractual duty to work Saturdays. The employer had reduced week-end staffing to the minimum, and had tried unsuccessfully to secure a voluntary replacement for plaintiff. The employer refused, however, to offer premium pay to induce others to assume Saturday work. Based upon the Union's objection, the employer also refused to reassign an unwilling senior worker to the Saturday shift. The Court held that the accommodation afforded was "reasonable," and stated that "TWA is not required by Title VII to carve out a special exception to its seniority system in order to help [an employee] to meet his religious obligations." Moreover, "reasonable accommodation" did not require an employer to pay overtime premium pay necessary to secure Saturday workers, as any cost beyond *de minimis* was an "undue hardship."

*Ansonia* found that the grant of three days paid leave for religious reasons and the right to take

unpaid personal leave was a reasonable accommodation. The employer's refusal to allow the employee to pay the cost of the replacement worker,
as an alternative to unpaid leave, or to require
that "business leave" be allocated for religious use
was not unreasonable. *Philbrook v. Ansonia Bd.
of Educ.* (2d Cir.1991).

In situations where any accommodation would
impose an "undue hardship," no accommodation is
required. For example, on days where the employee's presence is reasonably necessary, such as at a
retail store on its busiest day, the employer need
not excuse an employee. Such an accommodation
to the employee's Sabbath would cause an "undue
hardship." *Wisner v. Truck Central* (11th Cir.
1986).

If an employer uses an objective system, such as
seniority or rotation, for allocating week-end or
holiday work, Title VII does not require employers
to abandon the system. *Trans World Airlines, Inc.
v. Hardison,* supra. Indeed, the Act may prohibit
an employer from granting exemptions based on
the religion of the worker, because to do so would
discriminate against those employees forced to
work on an undesirable day solely because they
have no religious objection to such work. *EEOC v.
Ithaca Industries, Inc.* (4th Cir.1987).

## § 15.04  Exemption for Religious Organizations

The Act exempts religious organizations and corporations from the prohibitions against *religious* discrimination. This exemption is applicable to both the religious and the secular activities of the religious corporation. 42 U.S.C.A. § 2000e–1. For example, the Church operated a gymnasium that was open to the public. The gym discharged the plaintiff for failing to maintain his Church membership. This discharge fell within the exemption granted the religious corporation, and the exemption so applied to a secular business did not violate the "establishment clause" of the First Amendment. *Corporation of the Presiding Bishop v. Amos* (S.Ct.1987). A church operated school thus can impose its religion-mandated ethical standards on its employees. *Little v. Wuerl* (3d Cir.1991).

This exemption is available only to *religious corporations,* not to secular employers who seek to inject religious practices into the workplace. *EEOC v. Townley Engineering & Mfg. Co.* (9th Cir.1988).

## § 15.05  Labor Organizations

Title VII makes it illegal for labor unions to discriminate on the basis of religion, but the obligation to make "reasonable accommodation" for religious practices is limited to "employers." Nonetheless, the courts have imposed on unions the obligation to make accommodations. *International Ass'n of Machinists and Aerospace Workers, Lodge 751 v. Boeing Co.* (9th Cir.1987). Of unique concern to unions is their duty to accommodate religious objections of employees to payment of union dues imposed by collective bargaining agreements. If the employee's objection to dues payment rises to the level of being a bona fide "religious" objection, the duty to accommodate this belief requires either exempting the employee from the dues obligation, or providing the employee with a non-religious charitable alternative. The employee may not be discharged for exercising bona fide religious objections to union dues payments. The employee can be required, however, to pay the actual cost of services performed for the employee by the union, such as processing grievances under the collective bargaining contract. *International Ass'n of Machinists and Aerospace Workers, Lodge 751 v. Boeing Co.,* supra.

Use of compulsory dues for political activity over the objection of the worker violates the labor relations statutes, *Communications Workers v. Beck* (S.Ct.1988), and if imposed on public employees, violates the First Amendment right to be free from coerced support of expression. *Abood v. Detroit Bd. of Educ.* (S.Ct.1977).

# CHAPTER 16

# AGE AND THE AGE DISCRIM-
# INATION IN EMPLOY-
# MENT ACT

## § 16.01  Generally

Prohibition against age discrimination is found in the Age Discrimination in Employment Act, 29 U.S.C.A. § 621 et seq. (ADEA).  As the operative language of the ADEA was modeled after Title VII, similar terms of the two statutes are given a parallel construction.  *Western Air Lines, Inc. v. Criswell* (S.Ct.1985).  As does Title VII, the ADEA reaches all aspects of workplace discrimination: hiring, assignments, promotions, compensation, environment, and discharges.

The ADEA prohibits age discrimination against individuals who are at least forty years old.  Age distinctions applied to those *under* age 40, such as imposing a *minimum* hiring age of 18, 21, or 30, do not violate the ADEA.  However, a *maximum* hiring age, of say 35, is proscribed age discrimination if applied to a person over the age of 40.  The age 70 limit for protection was removed in 1986.  Consequently, *unless justified by a defense,* any fixed retirement age, 65, 70, or even 80, is a violation of the ADEA.

For those over age 40, younger persons are protected against age discrimination under the same terms as are older persons. It thus violates the ADEA to prefer a person 65 years old over one who is 45 years old.

It is age discrimination to impose on workers of one age group requirements or conditions not imposed on other age classes. An employer may not, for example, require employees over the age of 50 to take physical or mental tests not given to workers under age 50. Standards of performance and discipline must be applied equally to all age groups. *Shager v. UpJohn Co.* (7th Cir.1990).

## § 16.02  Proving Age Discrimination: The Title VII Models

Age discrimination can be proved utilizing the models of proof developed under Title VII. Supra, Chapts. 10 & 11. In summary:

### a.  *Direct Evidence*

If plaintiff presents direct evidence of age motivation, which the fact finder believes, the burden shifts to defendant to prove that the same decision would have been made for legitimate reasons. Absent such proof by defendant, plaintiff will prevail. *Wilson v. Firestone Tire & Rubber Co.* (6th Cir. 1991). The key is whether the words referring to age were said, and if so, whether the words are sufficient to create an inference of an age-motivated decision. When age references are "descriptive" and not "evaluative" (such as noting the ages of employees under review), the references create no inference of illegal age motivation. *Shager v. UpJohn Co.* (7th Cir.1990). Even "evaluative" remarks will not create an inference if they are "stray" comments, in that they were isolated or remote in time or connection to the employment decision. Compare *Beshears v. Asbill* (8th Cir. 1991) ("older employees have problems adapting to changes and new policies") with *Gagne v. Northwestern Nat. Ins. Co.* (6th Cir.1989) ("need younger blood"). Supra, § 10.02.

### b. Circumstantial Evidence: Disparate Treatment

Absent direct evidence, a plaintiff creates a prima facie case of age motivation through circumstantial evidence that includes unexplained disparate treatment. It involves three steps. If a qualified person over the age of 40 is rejected for a vacancy filled by a significantly younger person, or an older employee performing satisfactorily is dismissed while a similarly situated, but significantly younger, person is retained, this disparate treatment creates an inference of age motivation. *Hebert v. Mohawk Rubber Co.* (1st Cir.1989).

This evidence shifts to defendant the burden of presenting a "legitimate nondiscriminatory reason" for its actions. Mere denial of age motivation will not suffice. Failure to present a "legitimate," age-neutral factor will result in a judgment for plaintiff. If defendant presents a legitimate, non-discriminatory reason, the evidentiary burden shifts back to plaintiff to meet the ultimate burden of convincing the fact finder that the employer's decision was motivated by age factors. *Id.* Supra, § 10.03.

#### c. *Statistics*

Statistical evidence demonstrating a pattern of discharges of older workers can create an inference that such discharges were motivated by age. *Barnes v. GenCorp.* (6th Cir.1990). However, because disparities along age lines often can be explained by variables other than age, the statistics must show a "stark pattern" unexplainable on grounds other than age. *Rose v. Wells Fargo & Co.* (9th Cir.1990).

#### d. *Impact Analysis*

Impact analysis developed under Title VII is applicable to the ADEA. Proof of age motivation is not required. *Geller v. Markham* (2d Cir.1980). Plaintiff must first prove the impact of the challenged practice; impact cannot be assumed. *Wooden v. Board of Educ. Jefferson County* (6th Cir.1991) (crediting a maximum of 14 years experience not proved to have adverse impact on older workers). Plaintiff's burden may not be satisfied by proof that a challenged practice adversely affects a sub-class of persons over age 40; it must affect the entire over–40 class. For example, proof that a device adversely affects those over 60 is inadequate. *Lowe v. Commack Union Free School Dist.* (2d Cir.1989).

Upon proof of impact on the over 40 age group, defendant must prove that the challenged device is job related and is consistent with "business necessity." This burden is more than one of presenting evidence of job relatedness; it requires defendant to carry the burden of convincing the fact finder of the "business necessity" of the challenged practice. Supra, Chapt. 11.

## § 16.03  Specific Exceptions

### a.  Law Enforcement Officers and Firefighters

States or political subdivisions may refuse to hire any individual into, or may discharge any individual from, the position of a law enforcement officer or firefighter because of the individual's age *if* : (1) the individual is above a maximum hiring age or has reached the fixed retirement age; (2) these age limits are part of a statutory plan in existence on March 3, 1983; and (3) the plan was not a subterfuge to evade the purposes of the Act. 29 U.S.C.A. § 623(i). This exemption is effective through December 31, 1993, but may be extended by Congress.

## b. Tenured Professors

Until December 31, 1993, the Act permits compulsory retirement at age 70 of persons serving under contracts of unlimited tenure at institutions of higher education. Beginning in 1994, unless extended by Congress, professors will be protected against compulsory retirement based on their age.

## c. Executives

The Act permits compulsory retirement of an employee who: (1) has reached the age of 65; (2) for the preceding two years was employed as a bona fide executive or high policy maker; and (3) is entitled to an immediate, nonforfeitable annual retirement benefit from *this employer* of at least $44,000 per year. 29 U.S.C.A. § 631(c); 29 CFR § 1627.17; *Whittlesey v. Union Carbide Corp.* (2d Cir.1984) (attorney not a policy maker).

## d. Government Policy Makers

Similar to Title VII, the ADEA excludes from the definition of "employee" elected officials and "appointees * * * on a policymaking level." 29 U.S.C.A. § 630(f). Decisions made concerning government officials who are the first line advisors to elected officials are not "employment" decisions and thus are outside the scope of the Act. Consequently, mandatory retirement of high officials, such as state judges, at a fixed age does not violate the Act. *Gregory v. Ashcroft* (S.Ct.1991).

### e. *Apprenticeships*

[P]rohibitions contained in the Act will not be applied to bona fide apprenticeship programs which meet the standards specified [by the Department of Labor].   \* \* \* This is a recognition of the fact that apprenticeship is an extension of the educational process \* \* \*.

29 C.F.R. § 1625.13.

### f. *Other Federal Laws*

Age requirements imposed by other federal laws, such as "senior status" for federal judges, mandatory retirement of federal law enforcement officers and air traffic controllers, and age limits imposed by regulation on commercial air line pilots, have been upheld as indications of congressional intent to limit the scope of the ADEA. *Stewart v. Smith* (D.C.Cir.1982).

## § 16.04  Statutory Defenses

### a. *Seniority Systems*

Granting benefits based on relative seniority of employees is a time-based factor that could easily be equated with "age."   Nonetheless, an employer is permitted:

(A) to observe the terms of a bona fide seniority system that is not intended to evade the purposes of this Act, except that such seniority system shall not require or permit the involuntary retirement of any individual * * * because of the age of such individual.

29 U.S.C.A. § 623(f)(2).

The concept of "seniority" is the same under the ADEA as it is under Title VII, that is, "improving employment rights as length of employment increases." Supra, Chapt. 11. A "reverse seniority" system that *reduces* benefits and tenure with length of service does not meet the definition of "seniority." Cf. *Arnold v. United States Postal Service* (D.C.Cir.1988) (rotation of senior postal inspectors to major metro areas does not violate the ADEA).

The period to challenge the motivation for adopting or changing a seniority system is measured from the date the plan was adopted or altered, not from the date the system adversely affects the plaintiff. *Barrow v. New Orleans S.S. Ass'n* (5th Cir.1991). Cf. Civil Rights Act of 1991 § 112, Appendix.

### b. *The Bona Fide Occupational Qualification*

In language virtually identical to Title VII, the ADEA provides:

It shall not be unlawful * * * to take any action otherwise prohibited * * * where age is a bona fide occupational qualification reasonably necessary to the normal operation of the particular business.

29 U.S.C.A. § 623(f)(1).

The employer must prove that it has a factual basis for believing that all or substantially all persons over the age qualification would be unable to perform safely and efficiently essential, as opposed to peripheral, job duties. *Western Air Lines, Inc. v. Criswell* (S.Ct.1985). An older applicant may not be excluded because the job is deemed "strenuous" or demands "good health" based on the assumption that older persons lack those traits. Supra, Chapt. 8.

An employer can establish age as a BFOQ by proof "that some members of the discriminated against [age] class possess a trait precluding safe and efficient job performance that cannot be ascertained by means other than knowledge of the applicant's membership in the class. That is, there is a genuine threat to safety based on physical conditions that pertain to that age group, and it is impossible or highly impractical to deal with the older employees on an individualized basis." *Western Air Lines, Inc. v. Criswell,* supra. *Criswell,* sustained a lower court finding that under this standard the employer had failed to establish that age 60 was a BFOQ for a flight engineer on a commercial airline.

### c. *"Factors Other Than Age"*

Employers may "take any action otherwise prohibited * * * where the differentiation is based on reasonable factors other than age." 29 U.S.C.A. § 623(f)(1). For a "factor" to justify differential treatment it must be "reasonable" in that it has a relationship to bona fide employer purposes and is divorced from age considerations which, if applied generally, would undermine the purposes of the ADEA. "Reasonable factors other than age" include uniformly required credentials such as education, prior experience, and systems that measure merit or the quality or quantity of performance. So long as performance standards are uniformly applied, persons who do not measure up to those standards may be discharged "for good cause" regardless of their age. 29 U.S.C.A. § 623(f)(3).

The "factor other than age" proviso cannot be invoked if the "factor" is based on the passage of time to the detriment of the older worker. If, for example, an employer promotes a junior employee over more senior workers utilizing the factor "more time left on the job," this translates directly into the relative age of workers and would frustrate the statutory purpose of protecting older workers. *Geller v. Markham* (2d Cir.1980). Similarly, rejecting an applicant because he was "overqualified" is not a "factor other than age" because "too much experience, training, or education" is a time-related factor that exclusively affects older applicants, is not clearly related to job performance potential, and would insure the rejection of older applicants. *Taggert v. Time, Inc.* (2d Cir. 1991). On the other hand, favoring applicants with the *most* experience is a "factor other than age" because greater experience relates to an employer's genuine need to select the most qualified employees, and an "experience" credential does not undermine the purpose of protecting older workers.

While increased cost generally is not a "factor other than age" that can be used as a basis for discharging employees, *Metz v. Transit Mix, Inc.* (7th Cir.1987), relative salary demands may be the basis for *hiring* an inexperienced, younger applicant over an older, experienced applicant. *EEOC v. Atlantic Community School Dist.* (8th Cir.1989). Market forces can be a "factor other than age." Thus, salaries higher than those paid to incumbent workers doing similar work can be paid to attract younger professionals. *Davidson v. Board of Governors of State Colleges & Universities* (7th Cir. 1990). However, it will be age discrimination for an employer who pays higher salaries to attract new, and presumably younger, workers to not match bona fide offers made to older employees or applicants. Id.

### d. *"Bona Fide Benefit Plans": Cost Justifications in Making Age–Based Compensation Distinctions*

An employee benefit plan cannot be used to justify the failure to hire any individual or to require or permit the involuntary retirement of any individual because of age. Employers may observe, however, the *terms* of "bona fide employee benefit plans," such as retirement, pension, life insurance, disability payments, and health insurance. 29 U.S.C.A. § 623(f)(2). The EEOC has construed this provision to permit an employer to reduce benefits to workers based on age only to the extent that reduced benefits were justified by relevant differences in the cost. Consequently, reducing life insurance coverage as workers aged was permissible; reducing vacation time or sick pay was not because such reductions had no relationship to increased costs associated with aging. 29 CFR § 1625.10. A statutory exception is that health care benefits for employees and their spouses between the ages of 65 and 69 cannot be reduced upon their reaching age 65. 29 U.S.C.A. § 623(g).

EEOC guidelines also prohibit an employer from requiring employees to pay greater amounts to maintain equal benefits. An employer may, however, offer *voluntary* participation in a plan that permits the worker to maintain the same benefit level by increasing employee contributions if the voluntary employee contributions reflect the increased costs associated with aging. 29 CFR § 1625.10(d)(4).

*Public Employees Retirement System of Ohio v. Betts* (S.Ct.1989) rejected the EEOC's construction of the Act and held that age-based differences in a benefit plan need not be cost related and that a benefit plan is covered by the proviso unless the plan was used by the employer to discriminate in some nonfringe-benefit aspect of the employment relationship.

The Older Workers' Benefit Protection Act of 1990 superceded *Betts* and reinstated the EEOC interpretation. An employer may observe the terms of a bona fide benefit plan that makes age distinctions but only:

> where, for each benefit or benefit package, the actual amount of payment made or cost incurred on behalf of an older worker is no less than that made or incurred on behalf of a younger worker * * *.

EEOC Guidelines, which were incorporated by reference in the 1990 amendment, outline how such benefits are to be calculated.

## § 16.05  Reductions in Force

*a.  Generally*

A reduction in force violates the ADEA if it was prompted by a desire to eliminate older workers. *Johnson v. Minnesota Historical Soc.* (8th Cir.1991). However, reductions in force prompted by economic conditions which result in older workers being laid off, standing alone, does not create a prima facie case of age discrimination. The ADEA plaintiff in a work force reduction case must present direct, circumstantial, or statistical evidence that age was a determining factor in his job displacement. Absent such evidence the employer is free to reorganize and eliminate positions in whatever lawful manner it chooses. *Wilson v. Firestone Tire & Rubber Co.* (6th Cir.1991).

## b. Involuntary Layoff: Permissible and Impermissible Factors

The focus of the inquiry in a reduction in force is upon the reasons articulated by the employer for identifying the workers to be laid off. Unless justified by a defense, forced retirement based on age is illegal. "Years of service" or "pension eligibility" are inextricably tied to age and cannot be "factors other than age" that justify the layoff of older workers. *EEOC v. Altoona* (3d Cir.1983). The Act specifically permits employers to utilize seniority, laying off the most junior employees. Alternatively, the employer may devise an objective, non-age based system for determining which positions will be abolished, or the employer may adopt an objective system for evaluating performance of individual employees and base layoffs upon such evaluations. *Coburn v. Pan Am. World Airways, Inc.* (D.C.Cir.1983). An evaluation system cannot, however, utilize factors related to an employee's age, such as "future" or "potential."

As a general proposition relative salary may not be used to determine which workers to lay off. Higher paid workers are almost always the senior, older workers, and thus "high salary" is not a "factor other than age" that justifies the discharge of an older worker. *Metz v. Transit Mix, Inc.* (7th Cir.1987). A "failing company" has more leeway to use relative salaries. An employer may use relative pay to force retirement of older workers if the employer can establish that: (1) cost reductions are *necessary* to avoid liquidation; and that (2) forced retirement of the higher paid workers is the *least detrimental alternative* for the reduction of costs. *EEOC v. Chrysler Corp.* (6th Cir.1984).

Employees selected for involuntary layoff may be given severance payments based on non-age factors, but severance pay may not be denied to those employees eligible to receive vested retirement benefits because "pension eligibility" is a time-related factor and thus is not a "factor other than age." *EEOC v. Westinghouse Elec. Corp.* (3d Cir.1989). The 1990 Age Act amendments allow a partial set-off of severance payments against pension benefits, and provide a complex formula by which permissible reductions are calculated.

Older employees discharged because a reorganization eliminated their jobs must be given the opportunity to bid on available jobs. *Rivas v. Federacion de Asociaciones Pecuarias de Puerto Rico* (1st Cir.1991).

c. *"Voluntary" Early Retirement and the "Golden Parachute"*

The 1990 ADEA amendments allow special inducements to secure "voluntary" retirement if the inducements meet defined standards: (1) An employer may set a minimum age (e.g., 50 and over) for retirement eligibility, but may *not* limit inducements to a younger group, e.g., offering early retirement *only* to those age 55–60; (2) the employer may increase benefits called for in the employer's normal pension system through flat dollar incentives, enhancements tied to years of service, or a combination of age and years of service; (3) the employer may provide supplements to make up for lost Social Security benefits.

An employer cannot pressure an employee to accept retirement through threats of retaliation or indications that unless she elects to participate, she will be laid off without benefits. Such pressure, even if enhancements are accepted, is illegal mandatory retirement. *Hebert v. Mohawk Rubber Co.* (1st Cir.1989).

### d. *Insuring Voluntariness: Problems of Waiver*

Employers offering voluntary early retirement will seek to secure waiver of ADEA claims to avoid subsequent allegations that the retirement was involuntary. Such waivers are binding, even if imposed as a condition of participation in the retirement program, when they are voluntary *and* if they meet seven objective standards imposed by the 1990 amendments: (1) The waiver must be written in a manner calculated to be understood by the average individual; (2) the waiver must specifically refer to rights being waived under the ADEA; (3) it must not attempt to waive claims arising after its date of execution; (4) the employee must be given consideration for the waiver in addition to that which the employee is entitled to under existing pension or compensation schemes; (5) the employee must be advised in writing to consult an attorney; (6) the employee must be allowed at least 21 days to consider the agreement, or 45 days if the waiver is requested in conjunction with an exit incentive. Moreover, if the waiver is part of an incentive program, the employer must initially inform all of the eligible individuals about the program and its eligibility factors, job titles and ages of those eligible, and the ages of individuals in the same job unit who were not eligible; (7) the agreement must allow the employee seven days to revoke.

The burden is upon the defendant to prove that each statutory element has been satisfied. Failure to prove a valid waiver does not establish a violation of the ADEA, but only that rights which may exist under the Act have not been relinquished.

# CHAPTER 17

# HANDICAPS AND DISABILITIES

## § 17.01 Generally

Discrimination on the basis of physical or mental "handicap" is proscribed by the Rehabilitation Act, 29 U.S.C.A. §§ 706, 791–94. Moreover, the Americans With Disabilities Act of 1990, 42 U.S.C.A. § 12101 (ADA), provides, "No covered entity shall discriminate against a *qualified* individual with a *disability* because of the disability of such individual." § 102(a). The history of the ADA directed that it should be construed consistent with judicial interpretations of the Rehabilitation Act.

## § 17.02 "Disability" Defined

*a. "Impairment"*

The term "disability" under the ADA has essentially the same meaning as "handicap" under the Rehabilitation Act. A "disability" first requires a medically recognized physical or mental *impairment.* "Physical impairment" includes any "physiological disorder or condition, cosmetic disfigurement, or anatomical loss." Covered impairments include sight, speech, and hearing deficiencies; orthopedic and movement impairments including amputation; diseases such as cerebral palsy, epilepsy, multiple sclerosis, muscular dystrophy, diabetes, cancer, and heart defects. "Mental impairment" means "any mental or psychological disorder," and includes dyslexia, retardation, emotional illnesses, and learning disabilities. *Wynne v. Tufts University School of Medicine* (1st Cir.1991).

Contagious diseases, such as tuberculosis or HIV infection (the virus that causes AIDS), are physical impairments. *School Bd. of Nassau County v. Arline* (S.Ct.1987). The employer may discriminate against individuals with such diseases only by demonstrating that infected individuals constitute a significant risk to the health or safety of others, as for example in the food handling industry, that cannot be eliminated by reasonable accommodation. § 103(d); *Arline,* supra.

Alcoholism and drug addiction, to be distinguished from voluntary use and current illegal drug use, are defined disabilities, with the caveat that the ADA specifically permits employers to prohibit alcohol and drug use on the premises, may demand from drug users and alcoholics the same level of performance demanded of other workers, and may discriminate against employees involved in current illegal drug use. § 104. Employers may not discriminate against persons simply because they are alcoholics or are addicts completing a drug rehabilitation program. *Fuller v. Frank* (9th Cir.1990).

Because the physical or mental condition must be medically recognized, general physical or personality characteristics such as aggressiveness, *Daley v. Koch* (2d Cir.1989), minor obesity, *Tudyman v. United Airlines* (C.D.Cal.1984), or left-handedness, *de la Torres v. Bolger* (5th Cir.1986), are not protected "disabilities." The ADA specifically excludes some medically recognized conditions: homosexuality, bisexuality, transvestism, transsexualism, pedophilia, exhibitionism, voyeurism, gender identity disorders, sexual behavior disorders, compulsive gambling, kleptomania, pyromania, and psychoactive substance use disorders resulting from illegal drug use. § 511.

### b. *"Substantially Limit" "Major Life Activity"*

To be a "disability" the mental or physical impairment must *substantially limit* a *major life activity*. "Major life activities" include: caring for oneself, performing manual tasks, walking, seeing, hearing, speaking, breathing, learning, and having the ability to secure and retain employment. Thus, varicose veins, while unsightly and causing some pain, will be considered a disability only if they reach the level of prohibiting the individual from walking, standing, or holding regular employment. *Oesterling v. Walters* (8th Cir.1985). Partial loss of sight in one eye that does not substantially limit the ability of the person to see, to care for himself, or to secure work, is not a "disability". *Santiago v. Temple University* (E.D.Pa.1990).

The inability to work is a "major life activity," but the medical condition must "substantially limit" the ability to perform a wide range of jobs or tasks. Merely because an individual cannot perform a particular job does not render the individual "unable to work" and thus "disabled." For example, acrophobia limits the individual's ability to go into high places and thus prevented the plaintiff from holding a particular construction job, but the condition was not a disability because it did not "substantially limit" the plaintiff's ability to care for himself or secure a wide range of employment. *Forrisi v. Bowen* (4th Cir.1986).

An interference with a major life activity may be sufficiently transitory so as not to "substantially limit" that activity. A person with a knee injured in an accident is not "disabled" because the activity of walking is only temporarily suspended. *Evans v. Dallas* (5th Cir.1988).

### § 17.03 "Qualified Individual" and the Duty to Make Reasonable Accommodation

*a. Generally*

A person with a disability is protected against discrimination in hiring only if the person is "qualified." In construing the Rehabilitation Act, *Southeastern Community College v. Davis* (S.Ct. 1979) held that a person was "qualified" only if she could, with her hearing disability, perform essential functions of the position. Since the position of a nurse trainee required hearing ability, the deaf applicant was not "otherwise qualified." In another example the employer required secretarial workers to type 45 words per minute. A handicapped person who could type only 44 words per minute was not "otherwise qualified." *Lucero v. Hart* (9th Cir.1990).

Under the ADA a "qualified" person with a disability is one who has the "requisite skill, experience, and education requirements of the employment position, and who, *with or without reasonable accommodation,* can perform *essential* functions of such position." § 101(8). "Identifying essential job functions," and the potential to accommodate the disability to enable the individual to perform those functions, is part of the process of defining "qualified."

Unlike Title VII, where employers may not consider risks to the employee, in evaluating whether a person is "qualified" under the Rehabilitation Act the employer may consider risks of harm or injury to the employee. Thus, an employee who had an increased likelihood of falling and injuring himself caused by Parkinson's disease was not "otherwise qualified" to be a building inspector where the job required climbing around in buildings under construction. *Chiari v. League City* (5th Cir.1991).

*b.   "Essential Job Functions"*

If the person with a disability can perform all *essential* job functions, the disability may not be used to discriminate simply because the individual cannot perform some secondary or non-essential functions.  For example, if some occasional portion of the job might require lifting to a certain height, and the disability of the applicant made lifting to that height impossible, the applicant is "qualified" notwithstanding her inability to perform the minor job function.  Either structural modifications that eliminate the need for lifting or assignment of the occasional lifting to other workers would be required.

Even if essential job functions cannot be performed by the person with a disability, that person still is "qualified" if "reasonable accommodations" would enable the person to perform the essential functions.  Continuing the example, even where lifting is an essential portion of a job, the disabled applicant is "qualified" if reasonable accommodation, such as job realignment or structural alterations, would permit the disabled person to perform the job.

A job function is "essential" if the job exists to perform that function (such as reading would be an essential function of a proof reader), the function can only be performed by a few persons, or the function is specialized and the position is being filled to perform this particular function.  Thus, an essential function of a building inspector is climbing in buildings under construction. Accommodation does not require realigning duties to eliminate on-site inspections. *Chiari v. League City,* supra.

c.  *"Reasonable Accommodations" and "Undue Hardship"*

The ADA defines the term "discriminate" to include "not making reasonable accommodations to the known physical or mental limitations of an otherwise qualified individual * * * unless such covered entity can demonstrate that the accommodation would impose an undue hardship * * *." § 102(b)(5)(A). The ADA states that reasonable accommodation may include: (1) making existing facilities readily accessible to individuals with disabilities; and (2) job restructuring, part-time or modified work schedules, reassignment to vacant positions, acquisition or modification of equipment or devices, modification of examinations or training materials, and the provision of readers or interpreters. § 101(9).

"Undue hardship" means "significant difficulty or expense" considered in light of the overall resources of the facility, the number of persons employed, the effect on expenses or resources, and the impact of the accommodation upon the operation of the facility. § 101(10). The structure of the ADA places the burden on the employer to prove that a suggested accommodation would constitute an undue hardship. See *Mantolete v. Bolger* (9th Cir.1985). Providing sound amplification for a hearing impaired person or a large print monitor for a sight impaired worker would probably not constitute an "undue hardship" for most employers. An employer would be obligated to explore accommodating a blind applicant who is qualified by training and experience to perform the job of social worker, but who cannot read necessary legal documents. If providing a reader would require full-time service used only by the one blind employee, the expense may be such that such accommodation would constitute an "undue hardship." On the other hand, if providing a reader required only an occasional reassignment of another employee, the accommodation would not impose an "undue hardship." *Nelson v. Thornburgh* (E.D.Pa.1983). Even if an accommodation imposes considerable costs, the employer must consider the willingness of the applicant or a welfare agency to underwrite expenses.

## § 17.04  Motive under the ADA

The ADA and the Rehabilitation Act prohibit discrimination against those (1) with disabilities, (2) who have "a record of" such an impairment, or (3) who are "regarded as having" such an impairment. An employer who rejects a person because of a perceived disability in favor of an applicant who has no disability, violates the Act. If the employer asserts that the decision was based upon reasons other than the individual's disability (e.g., "poor personality"), the key issue is whether the disability or the neutral factor motivated the employer. That issue of motivation will be resolved similar to Title VII cases. *Smith v. Barton* (9th Cir.1990).

If the plaintiff presents direct evidence from the mouth or writings of the employer that plaintiff was rejected because of the disability, and convinces the fact finder that this animus played a significant role in the employer's decision, the burden shifts to the employer to prove that it would have rejected the plaintiff for legitimate reasons notwithstanding the disability. Supra, § 10.02.

In the absence of direct evidence that the employer was motivated by plaintiff's disability, plaintiff can create an inference of illegal discrimination by proving that: (1) She had a defined "disability"; (2) she was "qualified" in that she possessed the employer's stated educational and experience qualifications and could perform essential job functions with or without reasonable accommodation; (3) she applied for a vacancy and was rejected; and (4) the employer either hired a person without a similar disability for the position or continued to seek applicants.

Upon this proof the employer's burden is to present evidence of a legitimate, nondiscriminatory reason for rejecting the plaintiff (e.g., plaintiff had a criminal record, the person selected had superior education). Or, in a discharge case the employer may demonstrate that the disabled employee simply did not perform to the level of legitimate expectations uniformly imposed on workers.  *Jasany v. U.S. Postal Service* (6th Cir.1985).

If the employer presents evidence of a legitimate reason for its action, the burden reshifts to the plaintiff to persuade the fact finder that defendant was motivated by the plaintiff's disability.  Failure of plaintiff to carry this burden will result in a judgment for defendant.  Plaintiff need not prove, however, that his rejection was "solely" on the basis of his disability, only that it played a substantial role in the decision.  *Smith v. Barton* (9th Cir.1990).  Supra, § 10.03.

## § 17.05  Impact under the ADA

The ADA specifically defines the term "discriminate" to include "utilizing standards, criteria, or methods of administration that have the effect of discrimination on the basis of disability." § 102(b)(3).  Specifically, "discriminate" includes:

(6) using qualification standards, employment tests or other selection criteria that screen out or tend to screen out an individual with a disability or a class of individuals with disabilities unless the standard, test, or other selection criteria * * * is shown to be job-related for the position in question and is consistent with business necessity;  and (7) failing to select and administer tests concerning employment in the most effective manner to ensure that, when such test is administered to a job applicant or employee who has a

disability that impairs sensory, manual, or speaking skills, such test results accurately reflect the skills, aptitude, or whatever other factors of such applicant or employee that such test purports to measure, rather than reflecting the impaired sensory, manual or speaking skills of such employee or applicant (except where such skills are the factors that the test purports to measure).

Thus the ADA legislatively adopts judicially created impact analysis used under Title VII. Supra, Chapt. 11. For example, if an applicant for an equipment operator job is given a written test that he cannot complete because he suffers from the reading disability dyslexia, the employer cannot use this test to disqualify the applicant absent a showing that the test was a "business necessity" and that there was no non-written alternative to the test. *Stutts v. Freeman* (11th Cir.1983).

## § 17.06 Insurance and Benefit Plans under the ADA

The ADA permits observance of insurance and "bona fide benefit plans that are based on underwriting risks, classifying risks, or administering such risks that are based on or not inconsistent with State law." § 501(c). Thus, while an employer may not refuse to hire a qualified person with heart trouble, diabetes, or cancer based on fear of claims against insurance or disability benefit programs, the benefit program itself, following industry practice, may utilize bona fide risk distinctions. For example, as is common, the employer's insurance program may exclude from coverage pre-existing conditions or illnesses, or the plan may exclude certain disabilities such as alcohol or drug addiction. A program may provide a schedule of benefits that does not fully protect some disabilities, such as limiting the number of hospital days paid by the plan. *Alexander v. Choate* (S.Ct.1985).

## § 17.07  Medical Examinations and Inquiries

The ADA, unlike the Rehabilitation Act, sets forth specific standards for medical examinations and health related inquiries. Pre-employment medical examinations are forbidden, and inquiries are limited to questions concerning the ability to perform specific, job-related tasks. The employer may not ask about health, physical conditions, past treatment, or medication. To illustrate, applicants could be asked if they could lift fifty pounds (assuming this was a central job task), but could not be asked if they had "back problems" or "heart trouble."

After making a job offer, but prior to the employee starting work, employers may require a medical examination if: (1) all employees in the job category are given the examination; and (2) the results are maintained in separate, confidential files. The job offer may be revoked only if the disability discovered in the examination prohibits the employee, with reasonable accommodations, from performing essential job functions. For example, if an eye examination of a truck driver disclosed that the applicant could not safely drive a motor vehicle, the job offer may be revoked.

Voluntary post-employment medical programs are permitted provided that medical information is kept in separate confidential files. Mandatory post-employment medical examinations of employees will be unlawful unless they are job related and deemed to be a "business necessity." For example, employees in safety sensitive jobs, such as bus drivers, may be given periodic examinations to the extent their physical condition relates to their ability to perform safely. Such examinations could evaluate cardiovascular risks, eyesight, and hearing, but could not explore for conditions having no relationship to the safety of job performance.

Drug testing specifically is not a medical examination, and thus drug tests may be given to both applicants and employees without violating the Act.

# CHAPTER 18

## PROTECTION AGAINST RETALIATION: INDIVIDUALS WHO PARTICIPATE IN PROCEEDINGS OR OBJECT TO PRACTICES AS A PROTECTED CLASS

### § 18.01  Generally: The Statutes

Title VII, the ADEA, and the ADA, protect individuals (1) who have "made a charge, testified, assisted or participated in any investigation, proceeding, or hearing"; or (2) who have "opposed any practice made unlawful" by the Acts. The Equal Pay Act has similar protections. 29 U.S.C.A. § 215(a)(3). Although the statutes do not expressly protect federal employees against retaliation, the courts have implied such protection. *Ayon v. Sampson* (9th Cir.1976). Protection extends to employees or applicants based on the activities of a spouse or relative. *Aquino v. Sommer Maid Creamery* (E.D.Pa.1987).

### § 18.02  "Participation"

The prohibition against retaliation because of an individual's "participation" in proceedings or investigations extends to filing a charge or lawsuit, giving testimony, or gathering evidence in the anticipation of a proceeding, *Grant v. Hazelett Strip–Casting Corp.* (2d Cir.1989), including participation in state agency proceedings pursuant to the federal procedural mandates. *EEOC v. Kallir, Philips, Ross, Inc.* (S.D.N.Y.1975). Writing a letter to the EEOC complaining about the results of a hearing was considered a motion for reconsideration and thus protected "participation." *Pettway v. American Cast Iron Pipe Co.* (5th Cir.1969).

Allegations made during participation are absolutely protected in that an employer may not discipline an employee even for false and malicious statements. *Pettway v. American Cast Iron Pipe Co.,* supra. It is not unlawful retaliation, however, for an employer to file suit against the employee under state defamation law for statements made by the employee during non-judicial proceedings if: (1) recovery under state law requires proof of "malice", (2) the employer has a reasonable basis for eventual recovery, and (3) the suit was initiated for the purpose of vindicating the employer's good name and not to retaliate against the employee or to deter others from asserting rights under the statutes. *Bill Johnson's Restaurants v. NLRB* (S.Ct.1983) (construing NLRA).

## § 18.03   "Opposition"

The statutes protect most forms of lawful "opposition" to an employer's practices, including verbal objections to supervisors, filing complaints with civil rights groups or labor organizations, circulating petitions, publishing advertisements, making statements to the media, or engaging in concerted activity such as striking or picketing. *Payne v. McLemore's Wholesale & Retail Stores* (5th Cir. 1981).

The "practices" being opposed need not in fact be illegal. Opposition is protected if the employee has a reasonable belief that the employer's conduct was unlawful. *Jennings v. Tinley Park Community Consol. School Dist. No. 146* (7th Cir.1988). Where the employer's activity could not reasonably be construed to be illegal, opposition thereto is not protected. *Holden v. Owens–Illinois* (6th Cir.1986) (protest of non-implementation of affirmative action plan unprotected). Note, however, that "concerted activity for mutual aid and protection" is protected by the National Labor Relations Act, supra, § 2.01, and the speech of public employees on matters of public concern is protected by the First Amendment.

Opposition, unlike "participation," is not absolutely privileged. False and malicious public statements, *Hicks v. ABT Associates, Inc.* (3d Cir.1978), maligning the product of the employer, violations of the law, and unreasonable disruptions of the work of other employees are unprotected. *Hochstadt v. Worcester Foundation for Experimental Biology* (1st Cir.1976).

## § 18.04   Employer and Union Reaction

Any adverse action taken because of protected activity is prohibited. There is no need to prove an invidious animus. For example, it is unlawful retaliation for an employer to inform other employers that an individual filed discrimination charges, or to provide poor references based on the employee's protected activity. *Smith v. Secretary of the Navy* (D.C.Cir.1981). It is unlawful for a union to refuse to process a contractual grievance because a discrimination charge is pending with an enforcement agency. *Johnson v. Palma* (2d Cir. 1991).

## § 18.05   Proving Unlawful Retaliation

To make out a prima facie case of retaliation, plaintiff must show: (1) participation in protected activity; (2) knowledge of that activity by defendant; (3) an employment action disadvantaging the person engaged in the protected activity; and (4) a causal connection between the protected activity and the adverse employment action. A causal connection may be established either indirectly by showing that the protected activity was followed closely by discriminatory treatment, through evidence such as disparate treatment of fellow employees who engaged in similar conduct, or by direct evidence of a retaliatory animus. Once a prima facie case is established, the burden of production shifts to the defendant to articulate a legitimate, nondiscriminatory reason for its action. Should defendant meet the burden of coming forward with a permissible reason for its actions, the plaintiff must then show that the reasons advanced were pretextual. *Johnson v. Palma,* supra.

# PART IV

# COMPENSATION DISCRIMINATION

## CHAPTER 19

## THE EQUAL PAY ACT

### § 19.01  The Equal Pay Act Generally:  Scope

The Equal Pay Act, 29 U.S.C.A. § 206(d) (EPA), sets a standard for determining pay obligations to male and female employees.  Plaintiff must prove: (1) the work of the plaintiff was "equal" to the work of an employee of the opposite sex, (2) the work was performed in the same "establishment," and (3) the rate of plaintiff's pay was less than the rate paid to the employee of the opposite sex performing the equal work.  If plaintiff establishes these three facts, the burden shifts to the employer to prove that the pay difference was based on:  (i) seniority, (ii) a merit system, (iii) a system that measures quantity or quality of production, or (iv) "any other factor other than sex."  The burden of establishing one of these defenses is one of persuasion.  *Corning Glass Works v. Brennan* (S.Ct.1974). The equal pay obligation applies regardless of which gender is the victim of the pay difference. *Lyon v. Temple University* (E.D.Pa.1982). The EPA is not the exclusive remedy for sex-based pay discrimination; Title VII also proscribes compensation discrimination because of sex.

Pay discrimination based on race, national origin, or religion is not proscribed by the EPA but is proscribed by Title VII. Pay discrimination based on age is prohibited by the ADEA, and "disability" discrimination by the Rehabilitation Act and the ADA. The EPA reaches only sex-based *wage* discrimination. Other aspects of sex discrimination—hiring, harassment, job assignment, and promotions—must be remedied under Title VII.

## § 19.02    "Equal Work" Defined

*a.    Generally*

In enacting the EPA, Congress rejected a "comparable work" standard in favor of the more stringent requirement of "equal work". However, "equal" does not mean "identical." Work is "equal" if job duties are "substantially equal." *Thompson v. Sawyer* (D.C.Cir.1982). The focus is upon duties actually being performed, not motive, not artificial job descriptions. Discriminatory job assignments and work load discrimination violate Title VII, but if the jobs being performed by men and women in fact are unequal there is no violation of the EPA. *Waters v. Turner, Wood & Smith Ins. Agency* (11th Cir.1989).

## b. The Elements of "Equal Work"

The Act itself defines "equal work" as "jobs the performance of which requires equal skill, effort, responsibility, and which are performed under similar working conditions." "Effort" refers to the physical or mental exertion needed for performance. "Skill" is the ability that relates to the regular performance of job duties, not to abstract ability or unused potential. "Responsibility" is the degree of accountability required. It can involve: (i) supervisory responsibility over other workers, (ii) ultimate decision-making authority, or (iii) consequences directly attributable to performance of that particular job. For example, an employee who handles prescription drugs has more "responsibility" than an employee who sells non-controlled items. A bank teller who handles small deposits has less responsibility than one who manages large inter-bank transactions. *Brennan v. Victoria Bank & Trust Co.* (5th Cir.1974).

"Working conditions" is an industrial term of art. If conditions are not of the type industrial relations experts would use in setting salaries, they are not deemed to be "working conditions." The term, thus narrowed, encompasses the physical surroundings and hazards of a job, such as inside versus outside work, exposure to extreme temperatures, wetness, noise, fumes, toxic conditions, dust, vibration, risk of injury, or poor ventilation. "Working conditions" do not include the time of day, or shift, in which the work is performed. *Corning Glass Works v. Brennan* (S.Ct.1974).

All four elements of "equal work" must be satisfied. Elements may not be set off, or balanced, against each other. For example, one job requiring greater skill cannot be "equal" to a job that requires less skill but more physical effort. Job equality also requires qualitative equality. Regardless of equal *quantity* of skill, effort, or responsibility, two jobs of a different nature are not "equal." For example, one janitorial job required dusting and light mopping a large area, while the second involved heavy wet mopping of a small area. Both jobs required similar amounts of total work in that the two employees expended similar amounts of effort during a work period. However, because the qualitative *nature* of the effort expended was different, the jobs were not "equal." *Usery v. Columbia University* (2d Cir.1977).

When basic job duties are the same, additional secondary duties given one job render the work unequal only if five conditions are met. First, the additional duties are actually performed by each employee receiving the extra pay. Class-based premiums are not justified simply because some of the higher paid employees perform extra tasks. *Shultz v. Wheaton Glass Co.* (3d Cir.1970). Second, the extra duties are regular and recurring and consume more than a minimal amount of time. *Shultz v. American Can Co.—Dixie Products* (8th Cir.1970). Third, the extra duties are substantial as opposed to inconsequential. For example, the duties of turning off the lights, making coffee in the morning, and answering infrequent telephone calls do not make otherwise identical jobs unequal. *Hodgson v. Fairmont Supply Co.* (4th Cir.1972). Fourth, additional duties of a comparable nature must not be assigned to the lower paid employees. If, for example, the higher paid employee has the additional duty of carrying out trash at the end of the day, and the lower paid employee has an additional duty of restocking the soft drink machine, these additional duties off-set each other, making the overall jobs "equal." *Hodgson v. Brookhaven General Hospital* (5th Cir.1970). Finally, the extra duties must be commensurate with the pay differential. The employer cannot distinguish substantially equal jobs by assigning secondary duties to one employee if those additional duties normally are compensated at a lesser rate. *Shultz v. Wheaton Glass Co.,* supra; 29 CFR § 1620.20.

### § 19.03  "Establishment"

The EPA requires employers to provide equal pay for equal work of male and female employees only where the work is performed within the same "establishment." "Establishment" presumptively refers to a distinct and independent physical location. 29 CFR § 1620.9. The term is narrower than "employer" but broader than "department." For example, a retail enterprise may have five stores selling identical products, each in a different part of town.  Each store would be a separate "establishment."  However, departments within each store are not separate establishments even if distinctly identified or segregated within the store, and thus pay must be equal for equal work performed throughout the store.

Should the employer centralize its personnel and management operations and allow significant interchange of employees between the physical locations, the individual sites may merge into a single "establishment."  A school system with numerous separate schools, but with centralized personnel operations, is a single "establishment."  *Brennan v. Goose Creek Consol. Indep. School Dist.* (5th Cir.1975).

## § 19.04  Unequal Wage Rate

"Wages" refers to all aspects of compensation, including deferred compensation such as pensions or retirement and the value of "fringe" benefits such as health care benefits, vacations, and paid leave.  *Los Angeles Dept. of Water and Power v. Manhart* (S.Ct.1978).  Cf. 29 CFR § 1620.11 (payments for pregnancy leave are not "wages" which must be paid to men).  Premium pay for overtime and hazardous duty are also wages that must be provided male and female employees at the same rate.

The wage "*rate,*" as opposed to gross salary, must be calculated.  The "rate" can be a commission or piece rate. For example, a female manager of the female portion of a health club was paid a commission rate of 5% of female membership dues, and the male manager of the male portion of the club was paid a commission of 7.5% of male membership dues. Because more females joined the club than males, the gross incomes of male and female managers were nearly the same. Nonetheless, it is the "rate," not total wages, which determines an EPA violation, and the male and female managers were being paid at unequal *rates*. *Bence v. Detroit Health Corp.* (6th Cir.1983).

When the parties establish an hourly rate of pay, that rate must be equal for males and females doing equal work. If employees are paid a fixed sum based on relatively short time periods (weekly or monthly), the gross wages received should be translated into a per-hour rate. When salaries are set by reference to a longer period of time, such as a year, gross salaries generally should not be translated into an hourly rate.

## § 19.05 Making the Comparison

When not all members of the opposite sex doing equal work are paid at a rate higher than that paid the plaintiff, some courts compare plaintiff's wage rate to the *average* rate of members of the opposite sex doing equal work. *Heymann v. Tetra Plastics Corp.* (8th Cir.1981). Others identify an appropriate "comparator" of the opposite sex to which plaintiff's wage is measured and compared. *EEOC v. Liggett & Myers* (4th Cir.1982).

"[T]he Equal Pay Act applies to jobs held in immediate succession, as well as simultaneously." *Hodgson v. Behrens Drug Co.* (5th Cir.1973). Thus, a female "chief operator" was entitled to the same pay as the male "supervisor" whom she replaced and whose duties she assumed. Id. The two jobs need not even be held in immediate succession. A female employee was paid the same as her male immediate predecessor, but the male employee who preceded them both was paid more. The plaintiff may compare her job duties and pay rate to the remote predecessor, particularly if her training and experience more closely resemble the remote predecessor than they do the immediate predecessor. *Clymore v. Far–Mar–Co.* (8th Cir.1983).

## § 19.06  Defenses to Unequal Pay for Equal Work

### a.  The Enumerated Factors

Different pay rates can be based on a "system" of seniority, merit, or one that measures quality or quantity of work. It does not violate the Act to pay a male employee more than a female employee doing equal work if the difference is attributable to their relative length of service or to an established, objective evaluation system. The "system" must be uniformly applied to men and women, and must have been imposed in good faith without the intention of avoiding the remedial purposes of the Act.

If the pay difference was motivated by considerations of gender, it was sex, not the system, that accounted for the difference. From irrationality and informality flows an inference of sex-based motivation. *Brennan v. Victoria Bank & Trust Co.* (5th Cir.1974). However, merely because a system, such as seniority, disadvantages one gender does not deprive the system of its bona fides. The employer may thus use seniority as a wage setting factor in a work force where senior workers are men, with the consequence that men will be the highest paid employees.

The "system" need not be in writing, but it must be objective, rational, and regularly applied. Haphazard, idiosyncratic pay patterns are not justified by subjective, ad hoc, or post hoc conclusions that in each case the higher paid employee had more seniority or more "merit" than the lower paid employee. Even if the pay distinctions were reached in good faith, differences flowing from such conclusions are not the product of a "system." *Brock v. Georgia Southwestern College* (11th Cir. 1985).

### b. The Omnibus Defense—"Factors Other Than Sex"

The employer may justify the pay difference for equal work if the difference is based on "*any* other factor other than sex." If the factor is premised on sex or upon gender stereotyping, such as an assumed willingness of females to work for a lower rate, it cannot be a "factor other than sex." The "factor" cannot perpetuate past sex discrimination by the employer, as where the employer pays a night shift premium but has denied women the opportunity to work the night shift. *Corning Glass Works v. Brennan* (S.Ct.1974). However, merely because the factor results in statistically lower salaries for employees of one gender does deprive the factor of gender neutrality. *Kouba v. Allstate Ins. Co.* (9th Cir.1982).

"Factor" presupposes some level of objective rationality. On the other hand, to be valid the "factor" need not be as compelling as a "business necessity." *Kouba v. Allstate Ins. Co.,* supra. Some courts hold that a "factor" must derive from "unique characteristics of the same job; from an individual's experience, training, or ability, or from special exigent circumstances connected with the business." *Glenn v. General Motors Corp.* (11th Cir.1988). Others hold that a "factor" need only relate to genuine employer concerns, even if unrelated to employee performance or employer needs. *Kouba v. Allstate Ins. Co.,* supra. To illustrate the difference, an employer pays a bonus to workers who are the sole or primary wage earner for their families. "Head of household" will not be a valid "factor" if it must bear a relationship to the requirements of the job or to the individual's performance on the job. 29 CFR § 1620.21. However, courts which do not demand a strict relationship between the reason and employer-focused concerns sustain a "head of household" bonus on the basis of its general rationality.  *EEOC v. J.C. Penney Co., Inc.* (6th Cir.1988).

The costs of hiring workers of one sex, such as the need to maintain separate toilet facilities or the increased costs of pensions attributable to that gender, are not "factors" that justify lesser rates of pay to employees of that gender.  29 CFR § 1620.-22.

The number of "factors other than sex" is limitless;  a few examples include:

• *Shift Differentials.*  Payment of a different rate for the time of the day or the day of the week the work is performed is a "factor," which if uniformly applied and gender neutral will satisfy the "factor other than sex" defense. However, *if* females were denied the opportunity to work the shift that receives the premium pay, the differential attributable to that shift is based, at least in part, upon the sex of the employee, and thus cannot be a "factor other than sex."  *Corning Glass Works v. Brennan* (S.Ct.1974).

• *"Red Circle" Rates.*  When an employee in a higher paying job, because of exigencies of the employer's needs, is temporarily assigned to a lower paying position, the employer may "red circle" and continue to pay the reassigned employee at the previous, higher rate.  However, if the employer "red circles" a wage rate for a job from which one gender has been excluded, the "red circle" rate perpetuates prior gender discrimination and cannot be a "factor other than sex." *Corning Glass Works v. Brennan,* supra.

• *Temporary or Part–Time Work.* Economic needs of the employer and demands of the employees justify rates of pay for temporary or part-time workers that differ from rates paid the permanent work force, so long as the rates are uniformly applied to a non-discriminatory hiring pattern.

• *Education and Experience.* Superior education and experience are "factors" that an employer may reward. The education or experience receiving the premium must, however, have some relationship to the job of the employee and must be uniformly rewarded pursuant to a rational system. *Wu v. Thomas* (11th Cir.1988).

• *Training Programs.* A pay differential can be defended if the higher paid employee performing equal work is being trained for higher level jobs pursuant to a bona fide training program. The program cannot exclude or discourage one sex from participation, *Hodgson v. Behrens Drug Co.* (5th Cir.1973), and must be structured to provide rational training for higher level jobs. It will not be a "factor" if the program consists of unpredictable assignments dictated by the employer's day-to-day personnel needs. *Shultz v. First Victoria National Bank* (5th Cir.1969).

• *Salary Matching.* To recruit new or experienced employees an employer may match or exceed the salary that the person being recruited earns elsewhere. The salary rate at *another employer* is sufficiently rational to be a "factor." Prior salary is gender-neutral even though the higher salary level of male workers generally produces higher pay rates to males as a class. *Kouba v. Allstate Ins. Co.,* supra. Similarly, to keep an employee, the employer may match bona fide offers made by other employers. Salary matching can be a "factor other than sex," even if it appears that the outside offer was motivated in part by the gender of the employee. *Winkes v. Brown University* (1st Cir.1984). However, if the prior salary was established by the defendant and it was based initially on the gender of the worker, current salary rates based on the prior discrimination perpetuates the employer's discriminatory conduct and cannot be a "factor other than sex." *Bazemore v. Friday* (S.Ct.1986).

• *Profits.* An employer may pay premium rates to an employee based on the profit attributable to the *work of that employee,* and may pay different commission rates based on the profit margin of the *product or service* sold by the employee. If both genders are free to sell the product, the profit margin of the product is a "factor other than sex." Even the *general profitability* of the department or division in which the employee works has been sustained as a "factor other than sex" that justifies a higher rate of pay for all employees working in that department. *Hodgson v. Robert Hall Clothes,*

*Inc.* (3d Cir.1973). Courts which demand that a "factor" relate to the qualities of the employee or to the exigencies of the employer's business would reject departmental profitability as a "factor."

An employer established different commission rates for male and female employees in order to secure for each employee equal total remuneration. Remuneration equalization was not a "factor other than sex" because it was based upon the sex of the employee, not upon the product being sold. *Bence v. Detroit Health Corp.* (6th Cir.1983).

• *Legislation and Civil Service.* Sex specific legislation authorizing higher pay for women, but not men, who perform certain types of work, or who work during certain hours, cannot itself be a "factor other than sex." However, a gender neutral civil service law that defines distinct job classifications can be a "factor other than sex" for payments made according to the classification scheme. *Peters v. Shreveport* (5th Cir.1987).

## § 19.07  Employer Compliance

The EPA provides: "[A]n employer who is paying a wage rate difference in violation of [the Act] shall not, in order to comply with the provisions of [the Act], reduce the wage rate of any employee." 29 U.S.C.A. § 206(d)(1). "Any amounts owing any employee which have been withheld in violation of this subsection shall be deemed to be unpaid mini-

mum wages * * *." 29 U.S.C.A. § 206(d)(3).
Thus, if a violation has been established, the employer must: (1) raise the wage rate of the lower paid employee to that of the higher paid employee; and (2) pay the plaintiff the difference between what she earned and what the higher paid employee earned, plus statutory liquidated damages as provided by the Fair Labor Standards Act. Infra. Chapt. 27.

# CHAPTER 20

# COMPENSATION AND TITLE VII

## § 20.01 Title VII and the "Bennett Amendment"

One year after the Equal Pay Act was passed, Congress enacted Title VII which prohibits discrimination because of race, color, sex, national origin, and religion "against an individual with respect to his compensation." The potential overlap between the EPA and Title VII, to the extent that they both proscribed sex-based pay discrimination, is addressed by a proviso in Title VII, named after Senator Bennett:

It shall not be an unlawful employment practice under [Title VII] for any employer to differentiate upon the basis of sex in determining the amount of the wages or compensation paid * * * if such differentiation is authorized by * * * [the Equal Pay Act].

42 U.S.C.A. § 2000e–2(h).

This proviso addresses only pay differences "authorized" by the EPA, and pay differences are "authorized" by the EPA only if they fall within one of its four statutory defenses (seniority, merit,

186

quality and quantity, or "factor other than sex."). Thus, gender motivated pay differences violate Title VII even if the work of the male and female employees is not "equal" within the meaning of the EPA. *Washington County v. Gunther* (S.Ct.1981).

## § 20.02 Facial Distinctions under Title VII

### a. *Fringe Benefits and Actuarial Differences*

A facial compensation distinction between individual men and women or between individuals of different races or ethnic groups violates Title VII. In *Los Angeles Dept. of Water and Power v. Manhart* (S.Ct.1978) the employer required female employees to make larger contributions into a pension fund, and thus they received less current take-home pay than similarly situated male employees. The difference in treatment was based on the actuarial reality that women as a class have a longer life expectancy than men. To fund equal pension benefits to men and women, women had to pay more into the fund. The Court held that a different pension "pay-in" obligation between men and women is discriminatory, and is not made less so because, upon retirement, men and women as a class would receive similar pension benefits. Equal treatment of a *class* is no defense to different compensation paid to *individual* men and women. Moreover, mortality tables based on gender cannot be a "factor other than sex" because the mortality tables are expressly based on sex.

Pay-out distinctions in pension plans likewise are discriminatory and cannot be justified by class-based actuarial distinctions. *Arizona Governing Committee v. Norris* (S.Ct.1983) involved an employer that provided employees an optional tax sheltered annuity program in which employees could assign a portion of their salaries to an independent underwriter which held the employee contributions under the terms of a contract between the underwriter and the employee. These contracts provided as one retirement option an annuity for the life of the employee calculated according to a sex-based mortality table. Consequently, female retirees electing a life annuity, based on their projected longevity, would receive a lower monthly stipend than similarly situated male annuitants.

The Court held that *Manhart* was controlling. That the annuity was provided by an independent underwriter was not significant in that the benefit was based upon a contractual relationship between the employer and the underwriter, whereby wages eventually were returned to the employee in the form of deferred compensation. Consequently, the employer must be responsible for the eventual distribution of that compensation, even though it came from the hands of the underwriter. Second, providing the employee with non-discriminatory options, such as lump sum payment or an annuity for the life of both the employee and spouse, did not make the plan non-discriminatory where one option—the single life annuity—treated men and women differently. Finally, although the discriminatory payment was made to the individual *after* retirement, thus after the employment relationship ceased to exist, the pension annuity was a form of current, deferred compensation to an employee that falls within the scope of Title VII. Making different payments to similarly situated men and women was facial sex discrimination.

In sum, an employer need not provide fringe benefits or pensions, but if such benefits are provided, employers and the underwriters with which they contract must establish pay-in and pay-out obligations using race-neutral and sex-neutral formulae.

### b. Pregnancy Benefits:

Title VII defines "sex" to include:

pregnancy, childbirth, or related medical conditions; and women affected by pregnancy, childbirth, or related conditions shall be treated the same for all employment-related purposes, including receipt of benefits under fringe benefit programs as other persons no so affected but similar in their ability or inability to work * * *.

42 U.S.C.A. § 2000e–(k).

Employers need not have health care benefit programs. However, *if* an employer provides a benefit program, the program cannot exclude pregnancy and childbirth, or provide a level of protection for pregnancy and childbirth that is less than that provided for other similar medical conditions.

To illustrate, a health insurance plan with a general $100 deductible cannot impose a $200 deductible for pregnancy-related procedures. Medically necessary abortions and complications flowing from elective abortions must be covered in any benefit plan. The Act specifically provides, however, that a benefit plan need not provide benefits for "elective" abortions.

Health benefits need not be provided to dependents of employees, but if they are, the plan must cover pregnancy of employees' spouses at the same level of other health benefits provided dependents. *Newport News Shipbuilding and Dry Dock Co. v. EEOC* (S.Ct.1983).

If an employer provides leave, paid or unpaid, for general purposes, the Act requires that similar leave be provided for pregnancy and childbirth. An employer who provides disability leave for pregnancy is not required to provide an equivalent benefit to male employees. *California Fed. Sav. & Loan Ass'n v. Guerra* (S.Ct.1987). However, if *child care* leave, as opposed to pregnancy leave, is granted to mothers, child care leave must be afforded similarly situated fathers. *Schafer v. Board of Educ., Pittsburgh* (3d Cir.1990).

## § 20.03 Improperly Motivated Pay Decisions

Plaintiff will establish a violation of Title VII by proving that a compensation decision was motivated by race, sex, national origin, or religion. Proof of "equal work" for "unequal pay" between persons of different classes is one means of proving improper motive, but under Title VII proof of job equality is not required. *Washington County v. Gunther,* supra.

Improper motivation can be established by "direct evidence", such as documents or statements made by the employer that compensation was because of the race, sex, or national origin of the workers. If plaintiff proves that such illegal factors influenced salary decisions, the burden shifts to the employer to prove that the same salary would have been paid to the employee even in the absence of the illegal considerations. *Price Waterhouse v. Hopkins* (S.Ct.1989).

Absent direct or statistical evidence, an inference of illegal motivation is created by proof that persons from different classes perform work that is equal and receive unequal rates of pay. EPA analysis is used by analogy. Plaintiffs must prove that the work of the individuals from different classes was "equal" within the meaning of the EPA; job "similarity" is not adequate. *EEOC v. Sears, Roebuck & Co.* (7th Cir.1988). An inference of illegal motivation created by proof of unequal pay for equal work is refuted by defendant proving, not just presenting evidence, that the salary difference was a product of a neutral, legitimate reason, a burden that is similar, if not identical, to the burden placed on employers under the EPA ("factor other than sex"). *McKee v. Bi–State Dev. Agency* (8th Cir.1986).

Statistical comparisons showing that women earn on an average less than men, or that blacks earn less than whites, do not, standing alone, create an inference that the salary differences are the product of illegal motivation. Since salary differences can be attributed to many legitimate variables such as experience, job title, education, seniority, and performance evaluations, the elimination of chance as an hypothesis for the pattern of salary differentials does not lead to an inference that the pattern was influenced by race or sex. *Coble v. Hot Springs School Dist. No. 6* (8th Cir.1982). Nevertheless, a statistical technique known as multiple regression analysis can hold constant each identified "independent variable," and can produce a statistical conclusion that the illegal factor was the only variable that explains the observed salary pattern. The failure of plaintiff's statistical analysis to account for all possible variables is not fatal, as long as the evidence is sufficiently reliable for a court to conclude that it is more likely than not that impermissible discrimination exists. Possible omissions from the study do not require plaintiff's evidence be rejected. *Bazemore v. Friday* (S.Ct. 1986).

## § 20.04  Perpetuating Discriminatory Pay

An employer may not adopt salary practices which perpetuate previously used discriminatory pay rates. For example, an employer paid black employees less than similarly situated white employees. After the employer became subject to Title VII it provided salary increases of a similar percentage rate to minority and non-minority employees. However, because current wages, upon which percentage increases were based, were a product of past, albeit legal, discrimination, a percentage increase formula illegally perpetuated the prior discrimination. *Bazemore v. Friday* (S.Ct. 1986). Similarly, an employer who discriminatorily assigned female employees to lower paying jobs may not use their prior salary in those jobs to establish pay for women workers transferred to higher paying jobs. *Corning Glass Works v. Brennan* (S.Ct.1974).

## § 20.05 "Comparable Worth": Salaries and Impact Analysis

"Comparable worth" is a concept that persons who perform jobs objectively dissimilar should receive similar pay based on a finding that the jobs have comparable economic value to employers or comparable societal worth. Comparable worth theory posits that salaries set through market demands for particular types of jobs result in discrimination against women and minorities because of a history of their exclusion from higher paying jobs. Illegality of salary differences must, however, be established by proof of either illegal motivation or unjustified adverse impact of a neutral device.

Setting salaries by reference to market forces adversely affects those classes that have been traditionally excluded from full participation in the market. Nonetheless, impact analysis has been held inappropriate for application to compensation differences. Impact analysis is used to analyze factors that deprive groups of equal *opportunity* or equal job access; when each class is free to undertake higher paid occupations, the Title VII purpose of "equal employment opportunity" is satisfied. *AFSCME v. Washington* (9th Cir.1985). Even if impact analysis is theoretically appropriate, the "Bennett Amendment," 42 U.S.C.A. 2000e–2(h), allows employers to utilize any pay practice "authorized" by the EPA. The EPA, in turn, authorizes employers to base pay differences on "any factor other than sex," and external market forces that fix different salary rates for different jobs is a "factor other than sex" within the meaning of the EPA. *International Union, UAW v. Michigan* (6th Cir.1989).

To create an inference of illegally motivated pay discrimination, it is necessary for plaintiff to prove that the work he performed was "equal" to that performed by an employee of the opposite sex or different race. Mere "comparability" of jobs does not create an inference that different pay was a product of illegal motivation. Even if improper motive could be inferred from proof that two comparable jobs were compensated at noncomparable rates, an employer may refute such an inference by "articulating a legitimate, non-discriminatory reason" for the difference in treatment. Market demands for functionally different jobs is such a "factor", and it does not lose its legitimacy simply because, when used to set salaries, it adversely affects one race or gender. *AFSCME v. Washington,* supra.

# CHAPTER 21

# THE ADEA AND ADA
# CONTRASTED WITH
# TITLE VII

## § 21.01 The Age Discrimination in Employment Act

In language similar to Title VII, the ADEA prohibits compensation discrimination against persons over the age of 40 because of age. However, unlike Title VII, which precludes the use of actuarial tables or relative costs based on race or sex (supra, § 20.02(a)), the ADEA specifically permits employers "to observe the terms of a bona fide employee benefit plan such as a retirement, pension, or insurance plan." Such plans cannot be used as a basis for refusing to hire workers over age 40 or as a justification for their forced retirement, but the ADEA does permit different pay-out benefits based on age. Any such differences must, however, be premised on actuarial costs to the employer attributed to age differences. Supra, § 16.04(d).

## § 21.02 The Americans With Disabilities Act

The ADA prohibits discrimination in compensation against persons with disabilities. While an employer may make compensation differences based on job differences or job performance, the employer may not base pay differences on the physical or mental condition of the worker.  Similar to the ADEA, and unlike Title VII, the ADA permits employers to observe the pay-out terms of bona fide health benefit programs that provide different benefits for various medical conditions.  Such programs, however, cannot be used as the basis for refusing to employ qualified individuals with disabilities.  Supra, § 17.06.

\*

# PART V

# ENVIRONMENTAL DISCRIMINATION AND WORK PLACE RULES

## CHAPTER 22

## GENERAL PRINCIPLES OF ENVIRONMENTAL DISCRIMINATION

### § 22.01  The Statutes

Title VII, the ADEA, and the ADA make it illegal to "limit, segregate, or classify employees in a way which would tend to deprive any individual of employment opportunities" or to discriminate in regard to "terms, conditions, or privileges of employment." The statutes are not limited to economic or tangible discrimination, but "strike at the entire spectrum of disparate treatment." *Meritor Savings Bank, FSB v. Vinson* (S.Ct.1986). Forced transfers, denials of requested job assignments, even if there is no change in status or income, or assignments of overtime based on a race, national origin, age, or gender are illegal. *Paxton v. Union Nat. Bank* (8th Cir.1982).

The 1866 Civil Rights Act, 42 U.S.C.A. § 1981, applies to the formation and enforcement of the employment contract, including discriminatory terms in the original contract, but until amended in 1991 it did not prohibit post-contractual discrimination such as job assignments or work place harassment. *Patterson v. McLean Credit Union* (S.Ct.1989).

## § 22.02  Oppressive Atmosphere:  Segregation

Creation of an oppressive working atmosphere adversely affects a "term, condition, or privilege of employment."  Employer enforced segregation by race or national origin inherently creates such an environment, and thus discriminates in regard to a condition of employment. *Firefighters Institute for Racial Equality v. St. Louis* (8th Cir.1977).  Segregating the working area, changing areas, toilets, or eating areas according to race or national origin is illegal.  Employers may not sponsor or organize social or athletic events along racial or ethnic lines.  An oppressive environment also is created by an employer that directs Hispanic customers to Hispanic employees and Anglo customers to Anglo employees. *Rogers v. EEOC* (5th Cir.1971).  An employer has no affirmative obligation, however, to eliminate self-segregation of employees during their non-working hours in eating areas or at social events. *Domingo v. New England Fish Co.* (9th Cir.1984).

Sex segregation of toilet facilities and changing rooms does not violate Title VII because such segregation is consistent with societal norms of gender modesty and thus does not create a hostile or oppressive environment. Indeed, the employer's refusal to sex-segregate toilet and changing facilities could create a hostile working environment for female employees.

Unions may not segregate hiring halls or bargaining units by race or sex. *EEOC v. International Longshoremen's Ass'n* (5th Cir.1975). Employment agencies may not segregate their files, lists, or referral services. *Barnes v. Rourke* (M.D.Tenn. 1973).

As the 1991 Civil Rights Act amended 42 U.S.C.A. § 1981 to apply to "all benefits, privileges, terms, and conditions of the contractual relationship," this Act now prohibits racial segregation and harassment under the same terms as discrimination is proscribed by Title VII.

# CHAPTER 23

# GROOMING

## § 23.01 Grooming Standards as Religious Discrimination

The Title VII definition of "religion" includes "all aspects of religious observance and practice." If an individual's religious beliefs require observing grooming standards, such as facial hair on males, head coverings, or particular clothing styles, a rule that interferes with those dictates is prima facie discrimination because of religion.

The grooming standard can be justified by the employer's showing that an accommodation of the employee's religious practice would impose an undue hardship. Accommodation to a practice requiring facial hair imposes an undue hardship where the job requires wearing respirators which cannot be worn effectively by a person with a beard. *Bhatia v. Chevron U.S.A., Inc.* (9th Cir. 1984). If the job requires a distinctive uniform for purposes of identification, such as police officers or airline employees, significant exceptions to the prescribed uniform may impose an undue hardship. *Goldman v. Secretary of Defense* (D.D.C.1982). On the other hand, mere *esprit de corps* or a generalized desire to promote an "image" may not be sufficiently weighty to demand employee compliance with a grooming standard that conflicts with the employee's religious beliefs. *Isaac v. Butler's Shoe Corp.* (N.D.Ga.1980). Cf. *United States v. Board of Educ. for School Dist. of Philadelphia* (3d Cir.1990) (banning public school teachers from wearing religious attire was valid in light of the public school's need to maintain religious neutrality).

## § 23.02 Grooming Standards as Sex Discrimination

Requiring men to adopt a hair style not imposed on women (e.g., short hair) or imposing on women an obligation to wear a clothing style (e.g. a dress) not permitted on men is a facial distinction along gender lines. Nonetheless, different treatment of genders that conforms to societal standards of grooming does not burden either gender, and thus does not affect adversely a term or condition of employment. It is thus not discriminatory to require male employees to have neatly trimmed hair or to require all employees to wear "business attire," which for men is construed to mean a jacket and tie and for women a feminine suit or a dress. A weight-to-height ratio requirement for men and women that varies according to the natural weight differences between genders is not discrimination because neither sex is burdened differentially by the requirement. *Craft v. Metromedia, Inc.* (8th Cir.1985).

Grooming standards that impose a greater burden on one gender do adversely affect a condition of employment, and accordingly, are a form of sex discrimination. For example, if the employer requires female employees to remain svelt but allows male employees to become portly, this is sex discrimination because women are burdened more than men. *Laffey v. Northwest Airlines, Inc.* (D.C.Cir.1976). If women are required to wear skimpy or sexually provocative clothing that is humiliating or provokes sexual harassment from customers, the working environment of women employees is more burdensome than the working conditions of men. *EEOC v. Sage Realty Corp.* (S.D.N.Y.1981). Even if the uniform prescribed for female workers is not provocative, it is discriminatory where it reflects a sexual stereotyping that places women in inferior positions. For example, in *Carroll v. Talman Fed. Sav. and Loan Ass'n* (7th Cir.1979), the employer created a discriminatory working environment by permitting men to wear business attire of their choice while requiring female employees to wear an ensemble selected by the employer.

A rule that is burdensome and imposed *because of* the predominate gender of the work force is illegal sex discrimination notwithstanding the fact that all employees in the work force are of one gender. *Gerdom v. Continental Airlines, Inc.* (9th Cir.1982). Non-burdensome grooming rules are illegal when used as a pretext to discharge an individual because of membership in a protected class.

*Tamimi v. Howard Johnson Co., Inc.* (11th Cir. 1987) (requirement that women wear facial make-up was a pretext to discharge plaintiff because of her pregnancy).

## § 23.03  Language and Grooming as Race or National Origin Discrimination

A rule that prohibits speaking languages other than English at the work place, while not facially national origin discrimination, may adversely affect the working environment of persons from non-Anglo origins.  29 CFR § 1606.7.  Because of this impact the employer must justify an "English only" rule in terms of the rule's "business necessity."  Customer complaints about employees' use of a "foreign language" and the inability of supervisors to understand *private conversations* does make "necessary" a ban on employees conversing in their native language in private conversations. *Gutierrez v. Municipal Court* (9th Cir.1988).

Prohibiting a grooming style associated with a particular ethnic heritage does not necessarily create a burdensome environment for employees of that heritage.   *Rogers v. American Airlines, Inc.* (S.D.N.Y.1981) (prohibition of traditional "corn row" hair style was not race discrimination when applied to a black female).  A grooming rule will be invalid, however, if it is imposed as a pretext to discriminate against employees of a particular heritage or if it is not uniformly applied to all workers.  Moreover, a neutral grooming standard may adversely affect employment opportunities of a particular race. For example, a rule prohibiting facial hair has been shown to affect adversely black males because a genetically related skin condition which makes it difficult to shave affects a significantly higher percentage of black males. *Bradley v. Pizzaco of Neb.* (8th Cir.1991). Proof of its adverse racial impact shifts to the employer the burden of demonstrating the "business necessity" of its "no-beard" rule. *Woods v. Safeway Stores, Inc.* (E.D.Va.1976) (image of cleanliness of a food handler justifies no-beard rule).

# CHAPTER 24

# HARASSMENT AND CONSTRUCTIVE DISCHARGE

## § 24.01  Racial and Ethnic Harassment

A working environment charged with racial or ethnic hostility created or tolerated by the employer can violate Title VII. Such a hostile environment occurs when workers of a particular heritage are subjected to higher levels of supervision or criticism, regularly subjected to crude or practical jokes (whether or not racial in nature), or exposed to racial or ethnic insults, jokes or graffiti. Plaintiff must prove, first, that there were repetitive or debilitating incidents that would affect seriously the psychological welfare of a person of reasonable sensibilities. *Scott v. Sears, Roebuck & Co.* (7th Cir.1986). Rarely will a stray racial insult or an occasional practical joke rise to that level. *Hicks v. Gates Rubber Co.* (10th Cir.1987).

Second, plaintiff must prove that her work performance or psychological well-being was adversely affected by the environment. Regardless of how rough the atmosphere, the Act is not violated unless plaintiff proves that she was harmed by the environment. *Brooms v. Regal Tube Co.* (7th Cir. 1989).

Third, plaintiff must prove "employer" responsibility for the hostile environment. Hostile working conditions attributed to management personnel will be attributable directly to the "employer." Where the environment is a product of non-supervisory or co-worker harassment, it is attributable to the "employer" only if plaintiff proves that management officials knew, or reasonably should have known of the environment, and failed to take prompt, effective remedial action. *Hall v. Gus Const. Co.* (8th Cir.1988). Employers must make prompt investigations of harassment complaints and discipline those found to have engaged in harassment. A warning and reprimand may be adequate for first time, minor offenses. Transfer, denial of pay increases, layoff, demotion, or even discharge may be required for repeat or serious offenders. The employer may not remedy harassment by transferring the victim to more benign surroundings. *Guess v. Bethlehem Steel Corp.* (7th Cir.1990). Failure to take reasonable remedial action will ratify the harassing conduct by an employee.

## § 24.02  Sexual Harassment

### a. *"Quid Pro Quo"*

It is sex discrimination when an employer "conditions the granting of economic or job benefits upon the receipt of sexual favors from a subordinate, *or* punishes that subordinate for refusing to comply." *Chamberlin v. 101 Realty, Inc.* (1st Cir. 1990). As such "quid pro quo" discrimination involves actions by a person vested with supervisory responsibility, the exercise of that authority is attributable to the "employer." *Steele v. Offshore Shipbuilding, Inc.* (11th Cir.1989). Employee rejections of requests for sexual favors that produce adverse treatment need not reach a level of offensiveness necessary to create a hostile working environment; it is enough if tangible benefits were denied plaintiff because she rejected subtle overtures. Id.

An employee who secures a job because of her sexual relationship with a supervisor cannot claim gender discrimination when the supervisor demotes or fires her for inadequate job performance when their sexual relationship cools. *Freeman v. Continental Technical Services, Inc.* (N.D.Ga.1988). Thus, discrimination against an employee because the employee desires to promote or to maintain a sexual relationship is not a Title VII violation.

## b. *"Hostile Environment"*

A sexually discriminatory hostile environment is created by "unwelcome sexual advances, requests for sexual favors, and other verbal or physical conduct of a sexual nature," such as fondling or kissing. 29 CFR § 1604.11(a)(3). It can include graffiti, openly displayed sexually suggestive pictures, *Robinson v. Jacksonville Shipyards, Inc.*

(M.D.Fla.1991), and practical or tasteless jokes directed at one gender even though the conduct itself is not sexual in nature. *Hall v. Gus Const. Co., Inc.* (8th Cir.1988) (urinating in trucks used by female co-workers, "mooning," denying female workers use of equipment, spying on female workers while they used a toilet). A sexually discriminatory environment is created where supervisors engage in regular and open consensual romantic relationships with co-workers. *Drinkwater v. Union Carbide Corp.* (3d Cir.1990).

The conduct must reach the level of unreasonably interfering with the individual's work or of creating an intimidating, hostile, or offensive environment as measured from the perspective of a reasonable person of the victim's gender. *Ellison v. Brady* (9th Cir.1991). Therefore, the "normal" use of obscenity, isolated suggestions of sexual activity, or a single unwelcome touching will not rise to the level of infecting the working environment. *Rabidue v. Osceola Refining Co.* (6th Cir.1986).

The unreasonable environment also must be "unwelcome." *Meritor Savings Bank, FSB v. Vinson* (S.Ct.1986). A ribald atmosphere in which plaintiff fully participated does not violate the Act. *Jones v. Flagship International* (5th Cir.1986). Plaintiff's "voluntary" participation does not establish that the employer's conduct was "welcome." For example, a supervisor's embraces may be "unwelcome" even if they were tolerated without immediate protest. However, the defendant may probe plaintiff's failure to object, her past conduct with supervisors and others, as well as the victim's "sexual fantasies," to determine whether the activity of which the employee complained was "unwelcome". *Meritor Savings Bank, FSB v. Vinson,* supra.

Employers are not absolutely liable for workplace harassment. Liability is based on the application of common law rules of agency. *Meritor Savings Bank, FSB v. Vinson,* supra. Applying those rules, a supervisor with no immediate superior at the establishment who has power regarding the hiring, pay, assignment, and firing of workers at the establishment is the "employer" for the purpose of establishing liability for the hostile environment created by that supervisor. *Sparks v. Pilot Freight Carriers, Inc.* (11th Cir.1987). Moreover, harassment is imputed to the "employer" if the employer does not have a clearly expressed policy against sexual harassment and clearly stated, reasonable avenues for making harassment complaints known to management. Avenues of grievance cannot include an obligation to grieve to the harasser. *Meritor Savings Bank, FSB v. Vinson,* supra. Where such procedures are in place the employer is not liable for harassment by low level employees of which it was unaware.

To avoid liability, the employer which knew or should have known of the harassment must take prompt, effective remedial action. A reasonable response does not include transferring the victim to her disadvantage. Reprimands, reassignments, denials of scheduled pay increases, coupled with counseling may be adequate. Discharge of the offender is not always required. *Paroline v. Unisys Corp.* (4th Cir.1990).

## § 24.03 The Problem of Remedy and "Constructive Discharge"

Until Title VII was amended in 1991 a victim of harassment could secure no damages for pain, suffering, or even for medical expenses required to remedy the emotional trauma. Consequently plaintiffs often attached to their Title VII suit a pendent claim under state law for torts such as infliction of emotional distress, battery, and invasion of privacy for which damages can be collected under state law. See *Hall v. Gus Const. Co.* (8th Cir.1988).

Often an employee's immediate response to harassment is to leave the job, and thereafter seek reinstatement with the employer coupled with a demand for back pay for the period of unemployment. "When an employee involuntarily resigns in order to escape intolerable and illegal employment requirements * * * the employer has committed a constructive discharge." *Henson v. Dundee* (11th Cir.1982). An employee constructively discharged will be entitled to reinstatement, back pay with interest, damages, and as a successful party, an award of attorneys' fees.

"A constructive discharge exists if working conditions are such that a reasonable person in the

plaintiff's shoes would feel compelled to resign."
*Bruhwiler v. University of Tenn.* (6th Cir.1988).
Plaintiff must establish three elements: First, defendant has engaged in illegal conduct. Second the illegal conduct was "intolerable" to a reasonable person. This requires aggravating circumstances such as especially humiliating or unceasing harassment, assignment of demeaning or dangerous jobs, or a dramatic demotion. Third, the employee's action must be caused by, and in response to, the illegal conduct. An employee who resigns for personal reasons unrelated to her treatment has not been constructively discharged. *Henson v. Dundee,* supra. Most courts do not require proof of the employer's specific intent to force the employee to resign, but will find a constructive discharge when the employee's resignation was a reasonable and foreseeable response to the employer's illegal conduct. *Calhoun v. Acme Cleveland Corp.* (1st Cir.1986).

# CHAPTER 25

## SOCIAL RELATIONSHIPS

### § 25.01  Marriage and Nepotism

Federal law, unlike many state statutes, does not prohibit discrimination based on "marital status." However, it is race discrimination to make distinctions based on the race of an individual's spouse. *Parr v. Woodmen of the World Life Ins. Co.* (11th Cir.1986). Rules prohibiting the employment of spouses may be shown through statistical data to discriminate against the more traditionally low paid female employees. If such impact is proved, the anti-nepotism rule would have to be proved by the employer to be a "business necessity." The courts are divided on whether such a rule is justified. Compare *Yuhas v. Libbey–Owens–Ford Co.* (7th Cir.1977), with *EEOC v. Rath Packing Co.* (8th Cir.1986).

Nepotism will illegally perpetuate prior facial discrimination where an employer or union previously excluded blacks and continues to favor relatives of current employees or members. *Thomas v. Washington County School Bd.* (4th Cir.1990). Nepotism may also have an adverse impact on black applicants, as where a corporation is closely held by family members, and those family shareholders are given priority for promotions. Proof of impact shifts to the employer the obligation to prove that such a practice is a "business necessity." *Bonilla v. Oakland Scavenger Co.* (9th Cir.1982) ("business necessity" not proved).

### § 25.02  Sexual and Social Relationships

The courts are divided on whether it is sex discrimination for an employer to favor an employee or applicant with whom he is having a romantic relationship. Compare *King v. Palmer* (D.C.Cir. 1985) with *DeCintio v. Westchester County Medical Center* (2d Cir.1986). Similarly unclear is whether it is race discrimination to favor white workers for job assignments and promotions based on the fact that the white supervisor has a social relationship with the white applicant. Compare *Holder v. Raleigh* (4th Cir.1989) with *Roberts v. Gadsden Memorial Hosp.* (11th Cir.1988).

It is not sex discrimination to discharge a worker for having a sexual affair, so long as the rule is uniformly applied to both genders and all races. It is thus sex discrimination to discipline a female employee for having a sexual relationship if similar conduct of a male employee is accepted. *Duchon v. Cajon Co.* (6th Cir.1986). Cf. *Platner v. Cash & Thomas Contractors, Inc.* (11th Cir.1990) (dismissal of female employee for suspected affair with owner's son, who was also an employee, was not sex discrimination, but favoritism of a relative over a stranger). Discharging a black employee for having a social relationship with a white employee of the opposite sex, while raising no objections to social relationships between employees of the same race, is race discrimination.

Discrimination on the basis of an employee's pregnancy is a facial form of sex discrimination. Thus, to discharge a worker, whether or not she is the supervisor's lover, because the worker is pregnant is facially proscribed sex discrimination. Similarly, discrimination based on an employee's securing an abortion, whether voluntary or medically necessary, is a facial form of sex discrimination. 42 U.S.C.A. § 2000e–k. Discrimination against an employee because of divorce or remarriage, if premised on an employer's religious belief, is "religious" discrimination. *Little v. Wuerl* (3d Cir.1991).

# PART VI

# REMEDIES

## CHAPTER 26

## TITLE VII AND ADA REMEDIES

### § 26.01  Introduction to Remedial Powers

The Americans With Disabilities Act (ADA) adopts the remedial and enforcement provisions of Title VII.  Title VII provides that when the defendant

> [h]as intentionally engaged in * * * an unlawful employment practice * * * the court may enjoin the * * * practice, and order such affirmative action as may be appropriate, which may include, but is not limited to, reinstatement or hiring of employees, with or without backpay * * * or any other equitable relief as the court deems appropriate.

> 42 U.S.C.A. § 2000e–5(g).

In this context "intentional" means simply that the practice was not accidental; remedial power is not dependent upon proof that the statute was intentionally violated.  Although the statutory terms "may" and "with or without backpay" suggest broad discretion, in fact, the range of judicial discretion to deny or reduce back pay is very narrow.

Since proceedings are "equitable," courts exercise broad, flexible powers traditionally exercised by courts of equity, such as injunctions, appointment of special masters, conditional decrees, and reporting obligations. The power to enforce compliance with equitable decrees is through contempt proceedings.

Because proceedings are considered "equitable" courts refused to exercise the power to order "legal" damages. However, the Civil Rights Act of 1991 specifically allows for recovery of consequential monetary losses, and for compensatory damages for non-pecuniary injuries such as pain, suffering, inconvenience, and future loss of opportunity. The 1991 Act also allows punitive damages for malicious or reckless indifference to rights, but places caps on all *non-monetary losses*: $50,000 for "employers" of less than 101 employees, with a maximum of $300,000 for "employers" of more than 500 employees. No damages may be awarded if liability is based on adverse impact.

## § 26.02 Prospective Injunctive Relief: Hiring Orders and "Front Pay"

The Act specifically grants power to "enjoin the practice" and to order "reinstatement or hiring of employees." That power is routinely exercised. *Taylor v. Teletype Corp.* (8th Cir.1981). The fact that the victim has moved and is currently employed elsewhere does not justify denial of a hiring order. *EEOC v. General Lines, Inc.* (10th Cir.1989). If there is no vacant position to which the victim can be hired, courts usually will not order dismissal of an incumbent, but will order defendant to hire the victim into the first available position, and in the interim, pay the victim salary and benefits commensurate with the position illegally denied until the victim is hired into a substantially equivalent position ("front pay").

A court may deny a hiring order if discord, tension, or antagonism precludes effective job performance. In such cases the court will order payment of wages ("front pay") until such time as the victim secures substantially equivalent employment. *Berndt v. Kaiser Aluminum & Chemical Sales, Inc.* (3d Cir.1986). "Personality conflicts" or hard feelings engendered by the litigation do not justify denial of a hiring order. *Taylor v. Teletype Corp.,* supra.

The courts may order employers to cease illegal practices, such as the use of illegal selection devices. They may enjoin enforcement of illegal collective bargaining agreements, and order employers to correct employment records of victims. *Smith v. Secretary of Navy* (D.C.Cir.1981). Unions can be ordered to admit persons illegally rejected or to cease discriminatory referral practices.

## § 26.03  Back Pay

### a.  Extent of Discretion

Notwithstanding statutory language suggesting trial court discretion ("with or without backpay"), a successful plaintiff is entitled to an order requiring defendant to pay the wages and benefits it would have paid to plaintiff had it not been for the illegal discrimination. "Given a finding of unlawful discrimination, back pay should be denied only for reasons which, if applied generally, would not frustrate the central purposes of eradicating discrimination throughout the economy and making persons whole for injuries suffered through past discrimination." *Albemarle Paper Co. v. Moody* (S.Ct.1975). Good faith of the employer, uncertainty of the law, and even ambiguity in the position of federal enforcement agencies are insufficient reasons to deny back wages. Uncertainty in calculation is no basis for reducing back pay liability. Indeed, questions of ambiguity are resolved against the employer. *Salinas v. Roadway Express, Inc.* (5th Cir.1984).

Wage discrimination is a "continuing" violation in that each pay period constitutes a fresh violation of the Act. However, "[b]ack pay liability shall not accrue from a date more than two years prior to the filing of a charge with the Commission." 42 U.S.C.A. § 2000e–5(g).

### b. *"Good Faith Reliance" Defense*

Good faith reliance on official written opinions of the EEOC will serve as a defense to back wage liability. 42 U.S.C.A. § 2000e–12(b). Reliance on general guidelines addressed to the public at large, EEOC determinations of "no reasonable cause," statements made by the EEOC as a part of litigation, and informal advice received from an EEOC office do not fall within the good faith reliance defense. To avoid back pay liability, defendant's conduct must have been undertaken because of the written opinion and must in fact comply with the opinion.

### c.  Calculation of Back Pay

To "make whole" a successful plaintiff the court will order defendant to pay the total amount of compensation that the victim would have received had it not been for the illegal discrimination, including the value of fringe benefits and all uniformly granted pay increases. The statute requires deductions from this sum of all amounts actually earned during the period between the unlawful treatment of plaintiff and the date of the order. Social benefits, such as unemployment compensation, are not "interim earnings" that must be deducted from back pay. *Brown v. A.J. Gerrard Mfg. Co.* (11th Cir.1983).

The statute also imposes a mitigation obligation by stating that "amounts earnable with reasonable diligence shall operate to reduce the back pay otherwise allowable." 42 U.S.C.A. § 2000e–5(g). The burden is on the employer to prove: (1) in the geographical area there were positions available that were substantially equivalent to the job denied in terms of compensation, responsibilities, opportunities, and status, and (2) the victim did not exercise reasonable diligence in seeking out such positions. Plaintiff's mitigation obligation does not require seeking or accepting jobs significantly different from the one illegally denied. *Ford v. Nicks* (6th Cir.1989).

The amount of back pay is tolled at the point the victim accepts substantially equivalent employment, where the victim becomes unavailable for work because of illness or disability, or when defendant unconditionally offers instatement to the victim even if defendant's offer does not include remedial seniority running from the date of the illegal treatment. *Ford Motor Co. v. EEOC* (S.Ct.1982).

### d. Interest

Successful plaintiffs are presumptively entitled to prejudgment interest on back pay liability against non-federal employers and the Postal Service. Defendant's good faith or "close" questions of liability do not justify denial of interest. *Donnelly v. Yellow Freight System, Inc.* (7th Cir.1989). The 1991 Civil Rights Act allows interest to be collected against federal employers. *See Loeffler v. Frank* (S.Ct.1988).

## § 26.04  Damages

Illegal discrimination, particularly a discriminatory discharge, results in consequential losses, such as humiliation, economic dislocations, and loss of credit. Harassment often results in emotional and physical injury causing plaintiff to incur medical expenses. The broad authority in Title VII to "make whole" victims of discrimination suggested judicial power to remedy these injuries with legal damages. The courts uniformly held, however, that since Title VII proceedings are "equitable," courts lacked authority to award compensatory or consequential damages. *Shah v. Mt. Zion Hosp. and Medical Center* (9th Cir.1981). Similarly, the remedial nature of Title VII precluded the grant of punitive damages. The 1991 Civil Rights Act allows recovery of consequential losses, future pecuniary losses, and for nonpecuniary injuries such as mental anguish and inconvenience. The Act also permits awards of punitive damages for malicious or reckless disregard of rights. However, nonpecuniary losses are limited by a formula based on the number of employees employed by defendant. (Appendix, § 102(b))

Actions brought against state and local governments for violations of constitutional rights and actions brought for racially discriminatory denial of contracts under 42 U.S.C.A. § 1981 are "actions at law" that permit injured plaintiffs to recover damages; compensatory for actual loss, and punitive to punish and deter wanton or malicious violations of the law. *Johnson v. Railway Express Agency* (S.Ct.1975).

Unlike the Equal Pay Act and the Age Discrimination in Employment Act, Title VII and the ADA, have no statutory provisions for liquidated damages.

## § 26.05 Seniority

No less than with the denial of the remedy of back pay, the denial of seniority relief to victims of illegal discrimination in hiring is permissible only for reasons which, if applied generally, would not frustrate the central purposes of eradicating discrimination throughout the economy and making persons whole for injuries suffered through past discrimination.

*Franks v. Bowman Transp. Co., Inc.* (S.Ct.1976).

*Franks* ordered artificial remedial seniority running from the date of the discriminatory refusal to hire. The dissent argued that since the granting of artificial competitive seniority affected the rights of innocent incumbent employees, trial courts should have discretion to adjust competitive remedial seniority to consider the claims of incumbents. The majority rejected this scope of discretion, seeing the "complete relief" for victims of discrimination as more significant than the protection of seniority expectations of incumbent employees. Only in the most unusual of circumstances may a court deny the remedy of full seniority.

## § 26.06 Affirmative Action

The statute specifically directs courts to "order such affirmative action as may be appropriate." This authorizes judicial orders directing employers and unions to adopt racial, ethnic, or gender conscious affirmative action programs to remedy "persistent or egregious discrimination * * * where necessary to dissipate the lingering effects of pervasive discrimination * * * [or] pending the development of nondiscriminatory hiring or promotional procedures." *Local 28 of Sheet Metal Workers' Intern. Ass'n v. EEOC* (S.Ct.1986). Based on a "blatant and continuous pattern" of discriminating against blacks in hiring state troopers, the Court affirmed an order requiring the employer to promote blacks and whites at a 1–1 ratio until 25% of the officer corps were black. *United States v. Paradise* (S.Ct.1987). If the court is authorized to order race conscious affirmative action by virtue of past egregious or pervasive illegality, the court's discretion in fashioning a remedy is similar to the discretion that must be observed by employers voluntarily adopting affirmative action plans. That is, the affirmative action order must be reasonable, temporary, and not unduly trammel the interests of white employees or applicants. Courts cannot order employees fired or test scores altered; seniority systems may not be overridden to maintain a racial ratio. See supra, § 9.03.

Individual non-parties to the litigation may not challenge the propriety of an affirmative action order if they had notice of the order, an opportunity to object, or if another adequately represented them in the litigation and challenged the order on the same legal ground. (Appendix, § 108)

# CHAPTER 27

# REMEDIES UNDER THE EQUAL PAY ACT

## § 27.01 Generally: Back Pay

The Equal Pay Act (EPA), as an amendment to the Fair Labor Standards Act (FLSA), adopts the remedial provisions of the FLSA. The basic remedy is back pay, calculated as the difference in the rates of pay between the plaintiff and the person of the opposite sex who performed work that was "equal" to that performed by the plaintiff. This calculation is similar to back pay calculations under Title VII. Doubts as to how much is due to plaintiff are resolved against defendant. There is virtually no discretion for a trial court to deny a successful plaintiff full back wage recovery. *Laffey v. Northwest Airlines* (D.C.Cir.1984).

Similar to Title VII, an employer who relies in good faith on official written interpretations of the Act by the EEOC will not be subject to back wage liability. 29 U.S.C.A. § 259.

## § 27.02 Statute of Limitations

The cause of action accrues each day an illegal wage rate is paid to the employee. An action must be commenced within "two years after the cause of action accrues, except that a cause of action arising out of a willful violation may be commenced within three years * * *." 29 U.S.C.A. § 255. That is, a plaintiff can recover all illegally underpaid wages for a period of two years prior to the filing of the suit, or three years if plaintiff can prove that the violation was "willful." A violation is "willful" if "the employer either knew or showed reckless disregard for the matter of whether its conduct was prohibited by the statute." *McLaughlin v. Richland Shoe Co.* (S.Ct.1988).

## § 27.03 Liquidated Damages

In addition to back wages, a successful plaintiff is entitled to secure as liquidated damages an additional amount equal to the back wage liability. The right to liquidated damages is qualified to allow trial courts equitable discretion to reduce all or part of the *liquidated damages* —not back pay— if the employer proves that it acted in good faith *and* with reasonable grounds for believing that its actions were lawful. Neither compliance with industry practice nor absence of complaints from employees or the EEOC establish employer reasonableness. *Thompson v. Sawyer* (D.C.Cir.1982). However, the absence of challenges coupled with the reliance on advice of counsel can establish good faith and the reasonableness of the employer's pay system. *Hill v. J.C. Penney Co., Inc.* (5th Cir.1982). Even if defendant establishes its good faith and reasonableness, the court is not required to reduce the liquidated damages; proof of good faith and reasonableness merely *allows* the court to exercise its discretion to reduce liquidated damages. *Thompson v. Sawyer,* supra.

## § 27.04  Interest

Liquidated damages are a substitute for all other forms of monetary relief.  Thus when a plaintiff recovers full liquidated damages, plaintiff cannot recover interest.  Conversely, if defendant proves good faith and the reasonableness of its actions and the trial court exercises its discretion to deny plaintiff liquidated damages, the weight of authority allows plaintiff to recover interest on the back wage liability against non-federal employers. *McClanahan v. Mathews* (6th Cir.1971).

## § 27.05  Compensatory and Punitive Damages

Provisions for liquidated damages evince a congressional intent to make these statutory damages the substitute for the miscellaneous losses that generally comprise legal damages; compensatory, consequential, and punitive damages cannot be awarded.  *Slatin v. Stanford Research Institute* (4th Cir.1979).

## § 27.06  Injunctive Relief

Actions by private parties brought pursuant to 29 U.S.C.A. § 216(b) and by the EEOC under 29

U.S.C.A. § 216(c) are considered actions at law to secure retroactive back pay and, where appropriate, liquidated damages. Injunctions against future violations of the Act are available only if brought by the EEOC pursuant to 29 U.S.C.A. § 217. The court may enjoin future violations where the employer's conduct has been continuous and not inadvertent. *Hodgson v. Corning Glass Works* (2d Cir.1973). An EEOC action for injunctive relief may be joined with an action for back pay and liquidated damages filed pursuant to 29 U.S.C.A. § 216(c).

## § 27.08　Labor Organizations

While the EPA makes it illegal for labor organizations to cause or attempt to cause an employer to violate the EPA, 29 U.S.C.A. § 216(b) provides only that "employers" who violate the Act shall be liable to "employees". Consequently, private actions by employees may not be brought against labor organizations. *Northwest Airlines, Inc. v. Transport Workers Union* (D.C.Cir.1979). The EEOC has authority under 29 U.S.C.A. § 217 to enjoin illegal conduct by a labor union and to secure a decree subjecting the labor organization to back pay liability.

# CHAPTER 28

# REMEDIES AND THE AGE DISCRIMINATION IN EMPLOYMENT ACT

## § 28.01 Generally: The Statute and Extent of Discretion

The Age Discrimination in Employment Act (ADEA) incorporates, as does the EPA, the remedial provisions of the Fair Labor Standards Act (FLSA) subject to one caveat: "Liquidated damages shall be payable [under the ADEA] only in cases of willful violations of this Act." 29 U.S.C.A. § 626(b). In addition the ADEA provides: "In any action to enforce this Act the court shall have jurisdiction to grant such legal or equitable relief as may be appropriate to effectuate the purposes of this Act, including without limitation, judgments compelling employment, reinstatement, promotion, or enforcing the liability for amounts deemed to be unpaid * * * wages * * *." Id. This broad grant of equitable power is similar in scope to that granted by Title VII. Thus on most issues such as back wages, hiring, and reinstatement with seniority running from the date of illegal treatment, the courts follow the Title VII standard. There is very little discretion to deny such remedies to the successful plaintiff. *Dickerson v. Deluxe Check Printers* (8th Cir.1983).

## § 28.02    Hiring Orders and "Front Pay"

As the ADEA specifically authorizes hiring, reinstatement, and promotions, such remedies are granted except when extraordinary circumstances make the remedy inappropriate, such as where no vacancy is available or where discord, disagreement, and antagonism would undermine job performance. *Dickerson v. Deluxe Check Printers,* supra. Where such circumstances preclude a hiring order, courts generally award front pay equivalent to what the victim would earn in that position until substantially equivalent employment is offered the victim. *Maxfield v. Sinclair Intern.* (3d Cir.1985). That the victim has been granted liquidated damages, or is willing to accept front pay in lieu of reinstatement, is not grounds to withhold a hiring order. *Dickerson v. Deluxe Check Printers,* supra.

## § 28.03    Back Wages

Back wage calculation under the ADEA is virtually identical to the calculation under Title VII. Unlike Title VII, the ADEA has no express provisions requiring set-off of actual interim earnings and income that could have been earned by reasonable diligence. Nonetheless, mitigation in the form of set-offs is implicitly required. *Rodriguez v. Taylor* (3d Cir.1977).

## § 28.04 Liquidated Damages

Plaintiff may secure as liquidated damages an additional amount that equals the amount of back pay liability, if plaintiff can prove that the violation was "willful." "Willful" means that "the employer either knew or showed a reckless disregard for the matter of whether its conduct was prohibited by the ADEA." A violation is not willful simply because the employer "knew of the potential applicability of the ADEA." *Trans World Airlines v. Thurston* (S.Ct.1985). The courts are divided on whether an age motivated hiring or discharge is, by definition, "willful", or whether "willfulness" requires proof of malevolence or outrageousness. Compare *Dreyer v. Arco Chemical Co.* (3d Cir.1986) with *Lindsey v. American Cast Iron Pipe Co.* (11th Cir.1987).

The section of the ADEA applicable to federal employers does not incorporate the remedial provisions of the FLSA, but simply empowers courts to grant "legal and equitable relief as will effectuate the purposes of the Act." Consequently, liquidated damages cannot be collected against federal employers. *Smith v. Office of Personnel Management* (5th Cir.1985).

## § 28.05 Interest

Where liquidated damages are not awarded the courts uniformly allow, as under Title VII, prejudgment interest on the amount of back wages owing. Where violations are found to be willful and liquidated damages recovered, the courts are divided on whether interest is appropriate, whether it shall be awarded only on the back wages, or whether interest should be awarded on the entire amount, back wages and liquidated damages. See *Lindsey v. American Cast Iron Pipe Co.* (11th Cir. 1987). Interest may not be collected against federal employers.

## § 28.06 Damages

As courts have the statutory power "to grant such legal relief as may be appropriate to effectuate the purposes of the Act," compensatory and consequential damages appear to be authorized. Nonetheless, the courts have concluded that Congress, by providing for statutory liquidated damages, intended liquidated damages to be the sole source of monetary recovery for non-wage losses. Compensatory, consequential and punitive damages cannot be recovered. *Pfeiffer v. Essex Wire Corp.* (7th Cir.1982).

The provision of the Civil Rights Act of 1991 that allows recovery of damages, both compensatory and punitive under Title VII, was not extended to the ADEA.

# CHAPTER 29

# ATTORNEYS AND ATTORNEYS' FEES

## § 29.01  Appointment of Counsel

"Upon application by the complainant and in such cases as the court may deem just, the court may appoint an attorney * * * and may authorize the commencement of the action without the payment of fees, costs or security." 42 U.S.C.A. § 2000e–5(f)(1). Exercise of this authority is discretionary. The trial court will examine the merits of the claim, plaintiff's financial resources, and plaintiff's attempts to secure counsel, *Bradshaw v. Zoological Society of San Diego* (9th Cir.1981), but the court will abuse its discretion by denying a request for appointment of counsel solely because the EEOC failed to find reasonable cause to believe the charge of unlawful discrimination. *Slaughter v. Maplewood* (8th Cir.1984).

## § 29.02  Attorneys' Fee Awards: The Statutes and the Extent of Discretion to Deny a Fee Award

The common law rule in the United States is that each party is responsible for the fees of its attorneys, and need not compensate the prevailing party for the fees of its attorneys. The employment discrimination statutes uniformly alter this rule. Title VII and the ADA provide that "the court, in its discretion, may allow the *prevailing party,* other than the Commission or the United States, a reasonable attorney's fee as part of the costs * * *." 42 U.S.C.A. § 2000e–5(k). Attorneys' fees under the EPA and the ADEA are provided through the Fair Labor Standards Act which directs that "The court shall, in addition to any judgment awarded to *plaintiff,* allow a reasonable attorney's fee to be paid by defendant, *and* costs of the action." 29 U.S.C.A. § 216(b). The right to attorneys' fees under 42 U.S.C.A. § 1981 and § 1983 is granted by 42 U.S.C.A. § 1988 in language virtually identical to that in Title VII.

Notwithstanding discretionary language in the statutes, trial courts, in fact, have very limited discretion in determining whether a prevailing party is entitled to an award of attorneys' fees. "A prevailing plaintiff ordinarily is to be awarded attorneys' fees in all but special circumstances." *Christiansburg Garment Co. v. EEOC* (S.Ct.1978). A prevailing *defendant,* on the other hand, is entitled to an award of attorneys' fees only upon a finding that "plaintiff's action was frivolous, unreasonable, or without foundation." Id. As the ADEA and EPA provide for fees for prevailing *plaintiffs* only, it is doubtful whether attorneys' fees can ever be awarded to defendants under those Acts.

Attorneys' fees under the Immigration Reform and Control Act are recoverable "only if the losing party's argument is without foundation in law and fact." 8 U.S.C.A. § 2324(b)(j)(4)

Pro se plaintiffs are not entitled to an award of attorneys fees, even if the plaintiff is an attorney. *Kay v. Ehrler* (S.Ct.1991).

## § 29.03 Calculating Fee Awards

### a. *Generally: The "Lodestar"*

To be entitled to an attorneys' fee award plaintiff must be a "prevailing party." Plaintiff will be a "prevailing party" even if she is not successful on the central issue of the litigation, provided she succeeds on some significant claim that affords to her some of the relief sought. *Texas State Teachers' Ass'n v. Garland Independent School Dist.* (S.Ct.1989).

An attorneys' fee award is calculated by first identifying the number of hours reasonably expended by attorneys that are attributable to successful claims. That number is multiplied by a reasonable hourly rate. This produces a "lodestar" dollar amount, which may be adjusted to account for additional factors.

### b. *The Number of Hours*

As plaintiff must be a "prevailing party," plaintiff is not entitled to an award of attorneys' fees for time spent on distinct legal issues on which plaintiff did not prevail. Only if successful and unsuccessful claims share a "common core of facts" or are "based on related legal theories," may a successful plaintiff claim attorneys' fees for work done on unsuccessful claims. *Hensley v. Eckerhart* (S.Ct. 1983). Plaintiff may count not only hours spent in preparation for and participating in the judicial proceedings, but also those hours reasonably expended in exhausting necessary state or federal administrative procedures. *New York Gaslight Club, Inc. v. Carey* (S.Ct.1980). Plaintiff must document the number of hours expended, and in cases where there are both successful and unsuccessful claims, plaintiff must document the hours attributable to the respective claims.

## c. Hourly Rate

The hourly rate by which the number of hours is multiplied is the rate charged by attorneys in the community who have experience and background similar to that of plaintiff's attorneys. The rates actually or normally charged by plaintiff's attorneys will not control. *Save Our Cumberland Mountains, Inc. v. Hodel* (D.C.Cir.1988). Nor is the "lodestar" amount reduced by the fact that plaintiff's attorney works for a legal aid or civil rights organization that does not charge clients. *Blum v. Stenson* (S.Ct.1984).

## d. *Adjustments*

*(1) Contingency.* A "lodestar" amount may be enhanced by a multiplier where plaintiff's attorney had a contingency contract with plaintiff providing that the attorney would receive a fee only if plaintiff prevailed. To secure a contingency enhancement plaintiff must prove: (1) that competent counsel could not be secured without an enhancement; and (2) the amount of enhancement which the market allows for contingency arrangements. *Pennsylvania v. Delaware Valley Citizens' Council for Clean Air* (S.Ct.1987).

*(2) Expenses.* Overhead expenses such as utility costs and clerical salaries are subsumed in the attorney's hourly rate and may not be separately recovered. Expenses distinct from normal overhead which are billed separately from the attorney's time, such as long distance travel costs and compensation to law clerks and paralegals, may be recovered as attorneys' fees in addition to the lodestar amount. *Missouri v. Jenkins* (S.Ct.1989). Professional fees paid to consultants, such as statisticians or testing experts, who aid the plaintiff's attorney in the evaluation and preparation of the case, were not considered recoverable "attorneys fees." *West Virginia University Hospitals v. Casey* (S.Ct.1991). The 1991 Civil Rights Act provides otherwise.

*(3) Delay.* When litigation is protracted and the attorney's fees are paid only upon final resolution, the court may add an "interest" or inflation factor against non-federal employers, to account for the

long period of time in which the attorney received no compensation. *Missouri v. Jenkins* (S.Ct.1989). Alternatively, the *current* hourly rate, rather than the historical hourly rate will be used to calculate the lodestar.

*(4) Difficulty of Case, Skill of Counsel.* Generally, the difficulty of the issues presented will be reflected in the lodestar calculation and will not warrant an adjustment. Extraordinary skill of counsel, performing beyond the level of peers, and thus reducing the number of hours that would normally be expended, may allow some upward adjustment. Conversely, unusually poor performance may warrant a reduction in the award. *McKenzie v. Kennickell* (D.C.Cir.1989).

*(5) Amount of Recovery.* The amount of plaintiff's monetary recovery may not be used to reduce or limit the lodestar recovery. For example, a decree granting plaintiff $35,000 in back wages does not justify reduction of a lodestar calculation which would produce a $250,000 award of attorneys' fees. *Riverside v. Rivera* (S.Ct.1986).

\*

# PART VII

# ENFORCEMENT PROCEDURES

---

## CHAPTER 30

## TITLE VII AND ADA PROCEDURES: NON–FEDERAL DEFENDANTS

### § 30.01 Introduction and Overview

Under Title VII victims of discrimination may not simply file suit. Rather they must first exhaust complicated state and federal pre-suit administrative procedures. Thereafter, the EEOC may file suit in its own name or it may issue to the charging party a notice-of-right-to-sue. Upon receipt of this notice, the charging party has 90 days to commence a judicial action in a court of general jurisdiction. The Americans with Disabilities Act (ADA) incorporates the enforcement procedures of Title VII.

## § 30.02 Pre–Suit Requirements—The Charge

*a. The Nature of the Charge*

The charge is the document that triggers the legal process. The charge must be written and under oath. Personal appearance and oral allegations at the EEOC office will not suffice. *Schroeder v. Copley Newspaper* (7th Cir.1989). The charge must (1) name the individual alleging discrimination, (2) name the person or entity who allegedly discriminated, (3) outline the nature of the discrimination (e.g., hiring, discharge, compensation), (4) state the basis for the alleged discrimination (e.g., race, color, national origin, sex, religion, disability or retaliation), and generally (5) provide the time and place of the alleged discrimination. Considerable informality is permitted. Letters to the EEOC or completed EEOC "intake questionnaires," if they contain the requisite information, will suffice. *Clark v. Coats & Clark, Inc.* (11th Cir.1989). Amendments may remedy technical defects, such as lack of an oath or spelling of names, and may add specificity and clarification to the basic allegations. Such amendments relate back to the date of the original charge.

The charge sets the parameters of the legal complaint in that the ultimate law suit may only allege claims related to the charge. *Sanchez v. Standard Brands, Inc.* (5th Cir.1970). Thus, as a general proposition, only parties named in the charge are proper defendants, and only the discrimination charged may be litigated. Consequently, a law suit alleging sex discrimination cannot be premised on a charge which asserted race discrimination; a suit challenging a discharge cannot be based on a charge alleging pay discrimination. *Ang v. Procter & Gamble Co.* (6th Cir.1991).

*b. When and Where the Charge Must Be Filed*

*(1) The Time Periods.* Charges must be "filed" with the appropriate regional office of the EEOC.

*(a) Non–Deferral Jurisdictions.* In those few states which have no equal employment legislation, a charge must be filed with the EEOC within 180 days of the discriminatory act.

*(b) Deferral Jurisdictions.* In states or municipalities which have equal employment legislation substantially equivalent to Title VII and have administrative enforcement agencies recognized by the EEOC as empowered to enforce the local legislation ("Deferral Agencies"), the charge must be filed with the state or local agency, as well as with the EEOC. In these jurisdictions, Title VII contemplates a two step, sequential filing. A charge is first filed with the state agency. An EEOC charge may not be "filed" until state agency remedies have been "exhausted." Failure to comply with state time limitations will not prejudice federal statutory rights. So long as states are granted the *opportunity* to resolve the claim, the EEOC may entertain charges untimely under state law. Moreover, there is no requirement that a charge be filed with the state agency or with the EEOC

within 180 days, the time prescribed for filing EEOC charges in non-deferral jurisdictions. *EEOC v. Commercial Office Products Co.* (S.Ct.1988).

State agencies are granted a 60 day period of exclusive jurisdiction to investigate and attempt conciliation. If the state agency terminates its jurisdiction, either within or after the 60 day period of exclusive state jurisdiction, an EEOC charge *must be filed within 30 days* of the state agency's termination.

If the state agency has not earlier terminated its jurisdiction, a charge *may be filed* with the EEOC any time after the lapse of the 60 day period of exclusive state agency jurisdiction so long as the *filing with the EEOC is accomplished within 300 days of the discriminatory act.*

The two steps of filing, first with a state agency and then with the EEOC, need not be ritualistic. Informal agreements between the EEOC and local agencies have long relied upon a system of referrals. A charge originally deposited with the EEOC may be referred by the EEOC to the state agency. Referral of the charge will be deemed to be a "filing" with the state agency without the charging party having to formally present her own distinct state charge to the state bureau. After the state agency relinquishes jurisdiction, or the 60 day period of exclusive state jurisdiction lapses, the EEOC in practice "reactivates" the charge previously deposited with it. The charge is deemed "filed" with the EEOC at this point of reactivation. *Love v. Pullman Co.* (S.Ct.1972).

For purpose of calculating the 300 day period for filing charges with the EEOC, the charge will be deemed "filed" with the EEOC only upon the "reactivation" or refiling of the charge following completion of state proceedings or the lapse of the 60 day period of exclusive state jurisdiction. Consequently, in a case where a charge was first deposited with the EEOC 291 days after the discriminatory act, and was thereupon referred by the EEOC to a local agency which retained jurisdiction for the full 60 days allowed by Title VII, the EEOC charge was not timely. Notwithstanding its earlier deposit, the charge could not be "filed" with the EEOC until the lapse of the 60 day period of exclusive state jurisdiction, which occurred some 51 days after the 300 days allowed for filing a charge $(291 + 60 = 351$ days$)$. *Mohasco Corp. v. Silver* (S.Ct.1980).

State agencies may, however, voluntarily relinquish jurisdiction over the charge prior to the lapse of the 60 day period of state jurisdiction, even if jurisdiction is relinquished for the sole purpose of allowing a charging party to pursue federal rights. Should state proceedings be terminated within 300 days from the discriminatory act, a charge initially deposited with the EEOC and reactivated upon the state agency's termination would be timely. *EEOC v. Commercial Office Products Co.*, supra.

Formal "work share" agreements between local agencies and the EEOC *may* effectively permit a single filing with the EEOC. Such agreements provide that the state agency waives investigation of charges initially deposited with the EEOC. These agreements are self-executing and will instantaneously terminate state jurisdiction over charges filed with the EEOC. Consequently, in such jurisdictions there *may* be no need for the EEOC to refer the charge to a state agency and await either the lapse of 60 days or the formal termination of state agency proceedings. Where such agreements exist, a charge filed with the EEOC within 300 days following the discriminatory act *may* be timely. *Trevino—Barton v. Pittsburgh Nat. Bank* (3d Cir.1990).

In summary, to insure a timely filing in deferral jurisdictions, a charge should be deposited with a state agency or the EEOC prior to the lapse of 240 days from the discriminatory act. This permits deferral to the state agency, 60 days of state jurisdiction, and EEOC reactivation (or filing by the charging party) prior to the lapse of the 300 day limitation period. For a filing to be timely after 240 days, state agencies must voluntarily relinquishing jurisdiction over the claim prior to the expiration of 300 days. *Any charge filed after 300 days from the discriminatory act will be untimely.*

*(2) The Discriminatory Act.*   As timely filing of a charge is measured from the discriminatory act, the discriminatory act must be identified.   In hiring and promotion cases the time period begins to run from the date the charging party was rejected for the job for which she applied.   However, some courts hold that the period should not run until plaintiff is aware of sufficient facts to put a reasonable person on notice of discriminatory treatment, such as hiring a person of another class.   *Reeb v. Economic Opportunity Atlanta* (5th Cir.1975).   In discharge cases the statute begins to run on the date the charging party received unequivocal notice of termination, not the last day on the job. *Delaware State College v. Ricks* (S.Ct.1980).   While *Lorance v. AT & T Technologies* (S.Ct.1989) held that the time to challenge an improperly motivated seniority system is measured from the date the system was imposed, the Civil Rights Act of 1991, reverses *Lorance* and provides that the time to challenge such systems can also be measured from the point the plaintiff is injured by the application of the system.

Some violations are "continuing."   If a discrete act of a pattern of violations takes place within the limitation period, discrimination prior to the limitation period may be challenged.   For example, pay discrimination is a "continuing violation" in that each pay period constitutes a distinct illegal act.   A charge filed within 180 days (non-deferral state) or 300 days (deferral state) of the last pay period may challenge the pay system.   The Act permits recovery of discriminatory underpayment for a period of two years prior to the filing of the charge.   42 U.S.C.A. § 2000e–5(g).   Similarly, discriminatory working conditions, including harassment, are "continuing." If a discrete illegal act took place within the period for filing a charge, the complaint can include patterns of conduct that preceded the filing period. *Starrett v. Wadley* (10th Cir.1989). Finally, a number of related actions arising from a similar animus will be considered "continuing", such as where an employee is serially demoted to gradually more insignificant jobs, or repeatedly denied promotions or transfers. If the last discrete act fell within the limitation period, the entire pattern is subject to challenge. *Jensen v. Frank* (1st Cir.1990).

*(3) Tolling.* Limitation periods are not jurisdictional. *Zipes v. Trans World Airlines, Inc.* (S.Ct. 1982). Courts possess the equitable power to allow filings outside the statutory time limits. This power may be exercised on grounds of waiver or estoppel when acts of the defendant either threaten or lull the charging party into failing to make a timely charge. *Coke v. General Adjustment Bureau* (5th Cir.1981). The courts also may toll the statutory period based upon illness, erroneous advice from the EEOC, or grounds of basic fairness. For example, the time for filing an individual charge may be tolled during the period an individual was a member of a pending class action. *Snell v. Suffolk County* (2d Cir.1986). However, pursuing grievances under a collective agreement or filing suit under another statute does not toll Title VII statutory filing periods. *IUEW v. Robbins & Myers, Inc.* (S.Ct.1976).

## § 30.03   The Charge Before the EEOC

Once the charge is filed with the EEOC, following any deferral to state agencies, the EEOC has exclusive jurisdiction over the charge for 180 days. The EEOC is directed by the statute to notify the charged party.  The EEOC is also directed to determine if there is "reasonable cause" to believe the statute has been violated.  If so, the EEOC should attempt to eliminate such practices by "conference, conciliation and persuasion."  If after 30 days from the filing of the charge conciliation has not produced an acceptable result, the EEOC is free to file a complaint in court.  If the employer is a state or local government, the matter is referred to the United States Attorney General for possible legal action.  If the EEOC (or the Attorney General in cases involving state or local governments) elects not to sue, the charging party will be notified of the right to bring a legal action (notice-of-right-to-sue).

There is no statute of limitation on the EEOC's investigation and conciliation efforts.  Subject to reasonable limits, the charging party is free to await the outcome of EEOC proceedings.  Should the charging party desire to proceed as rapidly as possible, at any time after 180 days from the filing of the charge with the EEOC the charging party may request a "notice-of-right-to-sue."  If the EEOC has not filed suit during that 180 day period of exclusive jurisdiction, the EEOC will, indeed it must, issue the notice to the charging party.  *Rid-*

*dle v. Cerro Wire & Cable Group* (11th Cir.1990). A finding by the EEOC that there is no reasonable cause to believe a violation has occurred does not preclude issuance of the right to sue notice. *McDonnell Douglas Corp. v. Green* (S.Ct.1973).

## § 30.04  Filing of a Judicial Action

### a.  Public Suit

The EEOC (or the Attorney General if defendant is a state or local government) has the first option to file suit.  Prior to filing suit, however, the EEOC must notify the charged party and actually attempt conciliation.  *EEOC v. Klingler Elec. Corp.* (5th Cir.1981).  A suit may not be filed during the first 30 days following the filing of the charge.

If suit is not filed within 180 days the EEOC may lose its power to sue.  Should the charging party request a notice-of-right-to-sue at the end of the 180 days of exclusive EEOC jurisdiction, and thereafter file a private judicial action, the EEOC is precluded from filing an independent action.  Public agencies are limited to intervention in the private suit.  *Johnson v. Nekoosa—Edwards Paper Co.* (8th Cir.1977).

Title VII contains no express limitation on the time in which the government may file suit, nor is a limitation imposed by implication.  The EEOC need not file suit within the 180 days of its exclusive jurisdiction.  The EEOC is not governed by the time limitations imposed on suits filed by private parties.   State statutes of limitation are not adopted and imposed by analogy.  *Occidental Life Ins. Co. of Cal. v. EEOC* (S.Ct.1977).   Subject to the qualification that a timely private suit will preempt a government suit, and that the equitable doctrine of laches may ultimately bar litigation, the EEOC is free to file suit at any time.   The doctrine of laches can bar EEOC suits if the delay is inordinate, unexcused, and results in prejudice to the defendant.  *EEOC v. Great Atlantic & Pacific Tea Co.* (3d Cir.1984).

*b.   Private Party Suit*

*(1) Waiting Period, "Right-to-Sue" Notice.*   The prerequisite to any private suit is a notice-of-right-to-sue issued by the EEOC.   This notice will be issued by the EEOC when:   (1) The EEOC has completed its investigation of the charge but has determined not to file an action in its own name, even if the EEOC has determined that there is no reasonable cause to believe a violation has occurred;   or (2) the charging party has requested the right-to-sue notice after 180 days from the date the charge was "filed" with the EEOC.

Thus, the right-to-sue letter may be requested anytime after the EEOC has had 180 days of jurisdiction, but the charging party need not request the notice within any particular time period.   Subject to the defendant claiming laches, the charging party has a right to await the outcome of EEOC conciliation efforts even if these efforts take years. *Garrett v. General Motors Corp.* (8th Cir.1988) (waiting 14 years for right to sue notice barred by laches). After the lapse of 180 days from the filing of the charge with the EEOC, if the EEOC has not filed suit within that 180 day period, the EEOC must issue the right-to-sue letter when the charging party so requests.

*(2) Filing the Complaint.* From the date the charging party or his counsel *receives* the right-to-sue letter, the charging party has 90 days to "commence" an action in a court of competent jurisdiction (federal or state). This 90 day period to file suit is governed solely by reference to the date the EEOC letter was *received,* and not from the date of the discriminatory act.

To satisfy the statutory requirement that plaintiff must file a complaint within 90 days following receipt of the right-to-sue letter, plaintiff's judicial complaint must satisfy the pleading requirements of Rule 8(a)(2), Fed.R.Civ.Proc. ("A short plain statement of the claim showing that the pleader is entitled to relief.") While legalistic formality is not required, mere filing of the right-to-sue letter or petitioning the court for appointment of counsel, unless the papers outline the factual basis for the claim, will not be considered sufficient to satisfy Rule 8. *Baldwin County Welcome Center v. Brown* (S.Ct.1984). If the requirements of Rule 8 are satisfied, the complaint may be amended, with the amendments relating back in time to the original filing. Cf. *Schiavone v. Fortune* (S.Ct.1986) (relation-back not appropriate to add proper defendant unless the newly named defendant was actually served during the limitation period).

This 90 day limitation period is not jurisdictional, and as with the period for filing charges, it is subject to equitable doctrines of estoppel and tolling. For example, inaccurate advice from judicial officers or improper conduct of the defendant will permit the court to allow a filing outside of the 90 day period. Active pursuit of legal remedies that are frustrated by procedural requirements will allow tolling. *Crown, Cork & Seal Co. v. Parker* (S.Ct.1983), for example, permitted a putative member of a class action suit to file an individual suit after the class of which he was a member had been decertified by the court, even though more than 90 days had lapsed since the plaintiff received the right-to-sue letter. Equitable tolling does not extend, however, to "garden variety excusable neglect," such as where the charging party's lawyer was absent from the office when the right-to-sue letter was delivered. *Irwin v. Veterans Administration* (S.Ct.1990).

The right of a *private party* to file suit is not defeated by the EEOC's failure to perform its duty of notifying the defendant of the charge and undertaking conciliation. *Russell v. American Tobacco Co.* (4th Cir.1975).

## § 30.05  Class Actions

*a.  Private Actions and Rule 23*

Class actions are a procedural device allowed and governed by Rule 23, Fed.R.Civ.Proc. Class actions allow a representative to sue on behalf of numerous similarly situated individuals and are commonly used in civil rights litigation. The court cannot certify a class unless petitioner establishes four elements: (1) *Numerousity* —The persons petitioner seeks to represent are so numerous that their joinder as named plaintiffs would be impracticable; (2) *Commonality*—Common questions of law or fact exist; (3) *Typicality*—The claims asserted by the petitioner, or the defenses asserted against the claims, are typical of the claims existing in the class or defenses asserted against the class; (4) *Representation* —The named petitioner can fairly and adequately represent the unnamed class members in that counsel is qualified and there is no conflict of interest. *General Tel. Co. of the Southwest v. Falcon* (S.Ct. 1982).

If the trial court certifies the class under Rule 23(b)(2), the judgment rendered in that suit binds all members in the defined class. That is, individuals who were in the class cannot file subsequent suits to litigate claims raised in the prior class action litigation. *Cooper v. Federal Reserve Bank of Richmond* (S.Ct.1984).

To proceed under Title VII in a class action one of the named class representatives must have filed a timely charge with the EEOC and must otherwise satisfy the pre-requisites to suit. It is not necessary for class members to have filed a charge in order to benefit from any final judgment. Moreover, in the event that the class petition is denied or "decertified" for failure to satisfy the requirements of Rule 23, individual members will be free to invoke individual Title VII remedies, even if they failed to meet the strict time limitations imposed by Title VII. *Crown, Cork & Seal Co., Inc. v. Parker* (S.Ct.1983).

### b. Government "Pattern or Practice" Suits

Title VII specifically gives the EEOC the power to file suits challenging a private "pattern or practice" of illegal conduct. 42 U.S.C.A. § 2000e–6. This authority does not, however, permit the EEOC to proceed without exhausting the usual prerequisites of a charge being filed and conciliation being attempted. Power is granted to the Attorney General to sue state and local governments for "pattern or practice" violations. The government may proceed in such suits, in effect representing a large number of individuals, without securing class certification pursuant to Rule 23. *General Tel. Co. of the Northwest v. EEOC* (S.Ct. 1980).

## § 30.06 The Judicial Proceeding

The litigation of plaintiff's claims before the court is *de novo,* as opposed to a review of state or EEOC administrative proceedings. Thus, any finding by the EEOC may be admissible as evidence, but EEOC findings do not restrict complete readjudication of plaintiff's claims. *McDonnell Douglas Corp. v. Green* (S.Ct.1973).

Federal district courts are given subject matter jurisdiction of Title VII claims. Moreover, the failure of the statute to grant federal courts exclusive jurisdiction implicitly allows concurrent jurisdiction of state courts. *Yellow Freight System, Inc. v. Donnelly* (S.Ct.1990). As proceedings under Title VII were deemed "equitable" in nature, there was no right to a trial by jury. *Shah v. Mt. Zion Hosp. and Medical Center,* (9th Cir.1981). The Civil Rights Act of 1991 allows jury trials in Title VII actions seeking damages.

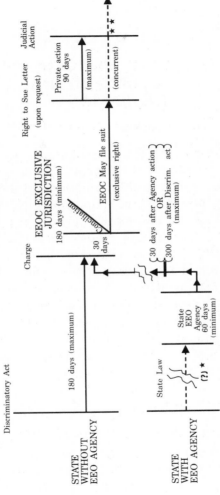

TITLE VII
NON-FEDERAL EMPLOYEE
PROCEDURAL CHART

★    State law will determine time for state agencies to hear claim. However, failure to comply with state law will NOT preclude federal filing according to the 300/30 day limit.

★★   Ninety day limit on private suit following right to sue letter is not binding on EEOC. EEOC may file suit subject only to laches.

|45A|

# CHAPTER 31

## TITLE VII PROCEDURES AGAINST FEDERAL DEFENDANTS

### § 31.01  Introduction

Enforcement procedures against federal employers are dramatically different. Primary responsibility for policing discrimination in the federal sector is placed on the employing agency. Each agency must have Equal Employment Opportunity Counselors. It is with these counselors, *not with the EEOC,* that the aggrieved federal employee first files a claim. The statute provides only that suit in federal district court *must* be commenced within 90 days (30 day's under prior law) of the receipt of the notice of final agency action, but *may* be commenced within 180 days from filing of the initial charge. The remaining procedures are largely a product of EEOC regulations.

### § 31.02  The Charge

EEOC regulations, 29 CFR Part 1612, require the aggrieved person to file a "pre-complaint" notice with a counselor within 30 days of the discriminatory act. Within a 21 day period the counselor is directed to attempt to resolve the dispute. If the charging party is not satisfied with the counselor's resolution, she may file a formal charge with "appropriate agency officials" who are usually a designated Equal Employment Director or Administrator. This more formal agency "charge" must be filed within 15 days following the "final interview" with the counselor.

## § 31.03   The Agency Determination

The agency will conduct an investigation of the formal charge. If unsatisfied with the recommendations flowing from the investigation, the charging party may ask for a determination by the agency head or may demand a formal hearing. The hearing, if demanded, will be conducted in an adversarial manner before a neutral administrative hearing officer. The findings of the hearing officer will be reviewed by the agency head (or delegate) and the charging party will be informed by letter of the final agency determination.

## § 31.04   "Appeal" of the Agency Determination

A charging party unsatisfied with the agency determination has an option: (1) file suit in federal district court, which suit must be filed within 90 days of the receipt of the agency's "decision letter," or (2) "appeal" the agency determination to the EEOC. An administrative appeal must be filed within 20 days of the receipt of the agency's decision letter. A supporting brief may be filed with the EEOC within 30 days of the filing of the appeal.

The EEOC will exercise appellate review of the record, as opposed to an independent investigation or adjudication of the claim. The EEOC has power to reverse or modify the agency determination. The charging party is free to file suit challenging the EEOC determination, and such judicial action must be filed within 90 days following notice of the final EEOC determination. *Mahroom v. Defense Language Institute* (9th Cir.1984).

## § 31.05  Judicial Review

While the federal plaintiff must "exhaust" internal agency procedures prior to filing suit, the charging party need not wait more than 180 days for agency procedures to resolve the claim. If after 180 days, no decision has been rendered by the agency, the charging party may (but not must) file a judicial action. Similarly, if after the final agency action, the charging party elects to file an administrative appeal with the EEOC, the charging must allow the EEOC an additional 180 days to conduct its review and issue a final decision. *Tolbert v. United States* (5th Cir.1990). After the lapse of 180 days of EEOC appellate jurisdiction the charging party may (but need not) file a judicial action. The charging party, however, must file his complaint in court within 90 days (30 under prior law) of the receipt of the EEOC decision.

The period in which to file the complaint runs from the date the notification letter is received by the charging party or by her attorney. The periods for filing a charge with the agency and for filing suit upon termination of agency proceedings are not jurisdictional and are subject to equitable tolling. Tolling will be appropriate where the claimant was actively pursuing the statutory rights or was tricked or mislead into missing a filing period. Tolling is not appropriate to remedy "garden variety of excusable neglect." *Irwin v. Veterans Administration* (S.Ct.1990).

The agency head, as opposed to the government agency, is the proper defendant and must be named in the complaint. Notwithstanding the often extensive administrative record, the district court does not simply review the record for error; plaintiff's claim is adjudicated *de novo*. *Chandler v. Roudebush* (S.Ct.1976).

Title VII is the exclusive remedy for federal employees alleging, race, national origin, sex or religious discrimination in employment. *Brown v. General Services Administration* (S.Ct.1976).

# CHAPTER 32

# EQUAL PAY ACT
# ENFORCEMENT

## § 32.01 Introduction: Equal Pay Act and the Fair Labor Standards Act

The Equal Pay Act (EPA) adopts the remedial and enforcement provisions of the Fair Labor Standards Act (FLSA). FLSA allows governmental enforcement through judicial actions filed by the Secretary of Labor. This power may be exercised in two ways: injunction suits filed under 29 U.S.C.A. § 217, or actions at law filed at the request of the employee pursuant to 29 U.S.C.A. § 216(c). The power to enforce the EPA was transferred by executive reorganization in 1978 to the EEOC. The Act also permits private law suits to collect unpaid wages. 29 U.S.C.A. § 216(b). That power remains unaffected by the reorganization, but the private suit must be filed prior to any suit by the EEOC.

Unlike Title VII, *the EPA has no requirement that charges be filed with the EEOC.* While the EEOC has authority to investigate alleged violations of the EPA, there is no obligation that the EEOC undertake conciliation of the claims.

## § 32.02  Statute of Limitations:  The Portal-to-Portal Act

Suits under FLSA, both public and private, are governed by statutes of limitations created by the Portal-to-Portal Act. 29 U.S.C.A. § 255. The Portal-to-Portal Act requires that FLSA suits be filed within "two years after the cause of action accrues, except that a cause of action arising out of a willful violation may be commenced within three years." "Willfulness" means that "the employer either knew or showed reckless disregard for the matter of whether its conduct was prohibited by the statute * * *." *McLaughlin v. Richland Shoe Co.* (S.Ct.1988). Thus in most cases employees can only collect back wages for a period of up to two years prior to the date the judicial action was filed in court.

As the Equal Pay Act does *not* require the employee to file administrative charges with the EEOC or to await the outcome of EEOC conciliation efforts, the employee or EEOC may simply file suit in a state or federal court, so long as the action is commenced within the two (or three) year period of the underpayment of wages.

Private suits under § 216(b) and suits by the EEOC brought pursuant to an employee request under § 216(c) are actions at law for which there is a right to a trial by jury.

# CHAPTER 33

## ENFORCEMENT OF THE AGE DISCRIMINATION IN EMPLOYMENT ACT: NON–FEDERAL DEFENDANTS

### § 33.01 Introduction and Overview

The Age Discrimination in Employment Act (ADEA) incorporates, with some modifications, the enforcement provisions of the Fair Labor Standards Act. Thus, both private and public suits are authorized. In addition, the ADEA adopts the statute of limitations found in the Portal-to-Portal Act. 29 U.S.C.A. § 626(e)(1). Thus, as with the Equal Pay Act, generally ADEA suits, both public and private, should be commenced within two years after the cause of action accrues, except if the violation is "willful".

Superimposed over this basic two year statute of limitations is an administrative charge requirement that is inspired by, but differs significantly from, the filing obligations in Title VII.

Executive reorganization in 1978 transferred authority of the Secretary of Labor to enforce the ADEA to the EEOC.

## § 33.02   Government Suits

As the EEOC utilizes power granted by the Fair Labor Standards Act, 29 U.S.C.A. §§ 216(c) and 217, and since that Act has no administrative or procedural prerequisites to a public suit, the EEOC may enforce the ADEA without any charges being filed with it or with state agencies. The only requirement is that the action be commenced by the EEOC within two years of the unlawful act (three years if the violation is willful). Thus, unlike Title VII which imposes no specific statute of limitations on the EEOC, the ADEA imposes a definite two year statute of limitations.

"Before instituting any action under this section, the EEOC shall attempt to eliminate the discriminatory practice * * * and to effect voluntary compliance * * * through informal methods of conciliation, conference, and persuasion." 29 U.S.C.A. § 626(b). The prior Act provided: "For the period during which the EEOC is attempting to effect voluntary compliance * * * the statute of limitation shall be tolled, but in no event for a period in excess of a year." 29 U.S.C.A. § 626(e)(2). This provision was repealed by the 1991 Civil Rights Act.

The right of any person to bring a private action under the ADEA terminates upon the commencement of an action by the EEOC. 29 U.S.C.A. § 626(c)(1).

## § 33.03  Private Actions

*a.  Introduction*

If the EEOC does not sue on behalf of the individual, that individual has the authority granted by FLSA to file a private suit. 29 U.S.C.A. § 216(b). The private suit is subject to the same two year statute of limitations applicable to EEOC, and it begins to run from the date of the discriminatory treatment. The ADEA, however, superimposes on private plaintiffs an administrative charge-filing obligation ("No civil action may be commenced by an individual * * * until 60 days after a charge * * * has been filed with the EEOC").

Such charge shall be filed

(1) within 180 days after the alleged unlawful practice occurred; or

(2) in a case [where a state agency is authorized to enforce age discrimination prohibitions] within 300 days after the alleged unlawful practice occurred, or within 30 days after receipt by the individual of termination of proceedings under State law, whichever is earlier.

29 U.S.C.A. § 626(d).

The content of the required "charge" is similar to that required under Title VII: a written document naming the parties and setting forth the nature of the alleged discrimination. *Supra,* § 30.-02(a).

The Civil Rights Act of 1991 requires the EEOC to notify the charging party when it terminates its proceedings and permits the charging party to file suit within 90 days of the receipt of this notice.

### b.  *Charge Filing in States Without Enforcement Agencies*

In jurisdictions not having agencies empowered to enforce laws against age discrimination (nondeferral states), a charge must be filed with the EEOC within 180 days of the discriminatory act. While not a jurisdictional requirement, the failure to file the charge in a timely fashion, unless excused by doctrines of equitable estoppel or tolling, will preclude suit.

## c. Charge Filing in States With Enforcement Agencies

*(1) State Charge.* The Supreme Court construed the statutory provision prohibiting the filing of suit until the expiration of 60 days after proceedings have been commenced under state law as an obligation on private plaintiffs to file claims with existing state anti-discrimination agencies. The Court held, however, that failure to observe state time limitations would not preclude filing of a federal claim, and that the state charge need not precede the federal EEOC charge. *Oscar Mayer & Co. v. Evans* (S.Ct.1979). Thus, unlike Title VII practice, the ADEA imposes on plaintiffs a simple exhaustion requirement. At some point prior to filing the judicial action, a charge must be filed with the state agency, and the state agency is granted 60 days to resolve the dispute. The state charge may thus be filed at any time: before, simultaneously with, or after the charge is filed with the EEOC.

*(2) The EEOC Charge.* A charge must also be filed with the EEOC. This charge must be filed within 30 days of the receipt of notice that a charge filed with the state has been terminated, or within 300 days of the discriminatory act, *which ever is earlier.* The EEOC charge may be filed prior to the state charge, simultaneously with the state charge, or subsequent to the state charge, so long as the filing meets the above 30/300 day time limitation.

## d.   *Waiting Period*

The charging party is required to wait for two 60 day periods to lapse: 60 days following the commencement of state proceedings *and* 60 days following the EEOC charge. These two periods can run simultaneously or overlap; the filing and the waiting periods need not be sequential.

While the EEOC is directed to notify the charged party and to attempt resolution of the charge through conciliation, the failure of the EEOC to comply with these directions does not preclude a private suit. The 1991 Civil Rights Act requires the EEOC to provide the plaintiff with notice when it terminates proceedings.

## e.   *The Suit: Two (three) Year Statute of Limitations or 90 days after notice:*

The time for commencing the judicial action is governed by the statute of limitations in the Fair Labor Standards Act. When the charge filing prerequisites are satisfied, and the two 60 day waiting periods are honored, suit should be filed within two years of the discriminatory act (three years if plaintiff can prove that the illegal conduct was "willful"). "Willful" is defined as "knowing" or "careless disregard." *McLaughlin v. Richland Shoe Co.* (S.Ct. 1988). Unlike Title VII procedures, which measure the time for filing suit from the date notice is received from the EEOC, one period for filing an ADEA suit is measured from *the discriminatory act.*

As an alternative to the two year limitation running from the discriminatory act, the Civil Rights Act of 1991 permits the charging party to file suit within 90 days after the EEOC notifies him that EEOC proceedings have been terminated. Thus, even if two years have lapsed since the discriminatory act, suit is timely if filed within 90 days from the receipt of the notice that EEOC proceedings have been terminated.

The right of a private party to file an ADEA suit terminates upon the EEOC filing suit. 29 U.S.C.A. § 626(c)(1).

ADEA claims can be filed "in any court of competent jurisdiction," federal or state. Trial will be *de novo,* without being limited by any state or federal administrative determinations. The ADEA provides for the right to a trial by jury. 29 U.S.C.A. § 626(c)(2).

There are no true "class actions" under the ADEA because provisions of the Fair Labor Standards Act, which apply to ADEA litigation, provide: "No employee shall be a party plaintiff to any such action unless he gives his consent in writing to become such a party and such consent is filed in the court in which such action is brought." 29 U.S.C.A. § 216(b).

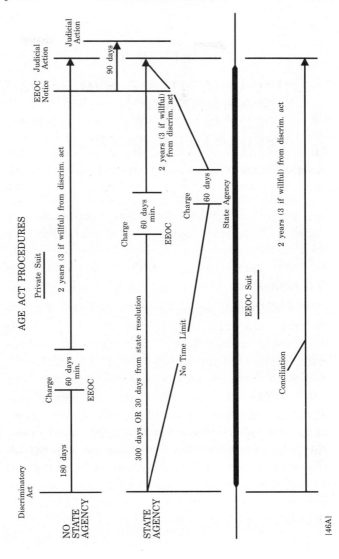

AGE ACT PROCEDURES

[46A]

# CHAPTER 34

# ENFORCEMENT OF THE AGE DISCRIMINATION IN EMPLOYMENT ACT AGAINST FEDERAL EMPLOYERS

## § 34.01 Introduction and Overview

Persons seeking relief against federal employers are subject to slightly different procedures than those seeking relief against private and state or local government defendants. ADEA procedures for federal employees also differ from those of Title VII plaintiffs.

The EEOC has no power under the ADEA to sue federal employers. Federal agencies are directed to provide administrative procedures to resolve complaints of age discrimination. These procedures, in fact, are very similar to those provided for resolution of Title VII claims. A plaintiff is free to invoke these internal procedures, but under the ADEA there is no obligation that such procedures be exhausted prior to filing a judicial action. The only pre-requisite to filing suit is the filing of a timely notice of intent to sue.

## § 34.02  Filing of a Charge

The ADEA permits, and EEOC regulations allow, the filing of complaints of age discrimination with the offending federal agency with an appeal to the EEOC.  29 CFR §§ 1613.511–1613.521.  The ADEA provides, however, that a federal plaintiff may commence a civil action if the individual provides the Commission "notice of an intent to file such action."  "Such notice shall be filed within 180 days after the alleged unlawful practice occurred."  Suit may not be filed until 30 days have lapsed since the filing of the notice with the EEOC.  Thus, a "notice" must be filed with the EEOC, and this notice must be filed within 180 days of the discrimination.

## § 34.03  Filing of a Suit

The charging party may pursue his claim within the federal agency procedures for resolving age discrimination claims, but there are only two prerequisites to filing suit: (1) filing notice with the EEOC of an intent to file a civil action within 180 days of the discriminatory act, and (2) waiting 30 days after the filing of the notice.  *Stevens v. Department of Treasury* (S.Ct.1991).

The time in which suit must be brought is unclear.  The two year statute of limitation applicable to non-federal employers does not expressly apply to claims against federal defendants.  The two year statute may apply by analogy, but two other possible statutory time limitations exist: (1) the general six year federal limitation for civil actions against the federal government, 28 U.S.C.A. § 2401(a); or (2) an analogous state statute of limitations. Without resolving which statute should be applied, the Court held that a suit filed one year and six days after the claim accrued was timely. *Stevens v. Department of Treasury,* supra.

## § 34.04   The Suit

The suit against the federal agency is *de novo;* any prior administrative findings are not binding on the court. There is no right to a jury trial in ADEA suits against a federal employer. *Lehman v. Nakshian* (S.Ct.1981).

# CHAPTER 35

# THE REHABILITATION ACT ENFORCEMENT

## § 35.01  Generally

Complaints of discrimination brought under the Americans With Disabilities Act (ADA) will invoke the procedures provided in Title VII. Procedures to remedy handicap discrimination claims against persons covered by the Rehabilitation Act differ depending on the basis of the coverage.

## § 35.02  Federal Employers:  § 501

Suits against federal employers are governed by the procedures applicable to federal employers under Title VII of the 1964 Civil Rights Act. 29 U.S.C.A. § 794(a)(1); Supra, Chapt. 31.

## § 35.03  Federal Fund Recipients:  § 504

If the employer is covered by virtue of its receipt of federal financial assistance, the individual will enforce the statute through procedures of Title VI (not VII) of the 1964 Civil Rights Act. 29 U.S.C.A. § 794(a)(2). There is an implied private right of action under Title VI, *Consolidated Rail Corp. v.*

*Darrone* (S.Ct.1984), and a jury trial may be available. *Smith v. Barton* (9th Cir.1990).

## § 35.04  Federal Contractors:  § 503

If coverage is based on the employer's service or supply contract with a federal agency, the individual must invoke administrative remedies. A complaint must be filed with the United States Department of Labor within 180 days of the discriminatory act. The Department of Labor will conduct administrative hearings on the complaint, and if it finds the contractor in violation of the Act, the Department of Labor may seek judicial enforcement of the contract between the agency and the federal government which prohibits such discrimination. 41 CFR §§ 60–741.26—60–741.29. The individual has no right to bring a private judicial claim against the federal contractor. *Howard v. Uniroyal, Inc.* (11th Cir.1983).

# CHAPTER 36

# PRECLUSION

## § 36.01  Prior Federal Adjudication

Concepts of res judicata prevent an individual from relitigating a claim or issue resolved in prior litigation. This basic rule is applicable to class actions. Class action judgments bind individuals who are members of the class. *Cooper v. Federal Reserve Bank of Richmond* (S.Ct.1984). Judgments in individual suits can have similar preclusive effects on subsequent EEOC actions on behalf of the same individuals, and EEOC suits on behalf of an individual will prohibit the individual from relitigating issues raised on his behalf by the EEOC. *EEOC v. U.S. Steel Corp.* (3d Cir.1990).

Resolution of issues in suits filed under parallel statutes preclude litigating the same facts or issues under other statutes. For example, an individual who claims a racially motivated refusal to hire under 42 U.S.C.A. § 1981 is precluded from relitigating the same factual claim under Title VII. *Lincoln v. Board of Regents* (11th Cir.1983). However, an individual not a party to prior litigation is not bound by the judgment even if the individual was aware of the litigation and could have intervened therein. For example, a race discrimination suit filed by black employees resulted in a judgment and affirmative action remedial order in favor of the plaintiffs. Subsequently, white incumbent employees, because they were not parties in the race discrimination suit, were permitted to challenge the legality of the affirmative action remedy which adversely affected them. *Martin v. Wilks* (S.Ct.1989). Cf. 1991 Civil Rights Act.

## § 36.02  Prior State Adjudication

State *agency* determinations on charges filed with them pursuant to Title VII or the ADEA do not preclude subsequent federal court adjudication of the claims. *Astoria Federal Sav. & Loan Ass'n v. Solimino* (S.Ct.1991). However, 28 U.S.C.A. § 1738 requires federal courts to give preclusive effect to state *judicial determinations* to the extent that the determinations would be preclusive in subsequent state judicial proceedings. Thus *judicially reviewed* findings by state administrative agencies, if preclusive in state courts, will preclude federal claims based on facts resolved in the state administrative proceeding. *Kremer v. Chemical Const. Corp.* (S.Ct.1982).

## § 36.03  Grievance Arbitration

An employee who has contractually agreed to submit a discharge claim to arbitration cannot refuse to honor that contractual obligation even though the employee is asserting that the discharge violated federal fair employment law. *Gilmer v. Interstate/Johnson Lane Corp.* (S.Ct.1991). However, resolution through arbitration of claims filed under collective bargaining agreements will not preclude subsequent litigation of statutory claims; factual findings of an arbitrator are not binding on the court. *Alexander v. Gardner—Denver Co.* (S.Ct.1974). The courts are divided, however, on whether judicial confirmation of an arbitration award will preclude subsequent litigation of the factual issues resolved by the arbitrator. *Bottini v. Sadore Management Corp.* (2d Cir.1985).

\*

# APPENDIX

# THE CIVIL RIGHTS ACT OF 1991

The Civil Rights Act of 1991 was signed by President Bush on November 21, 1991, and became effective on that date. This Act was the product of the compromise which followed the veto of the earlier, and in most ways quite similar, Act. The 1991 Act has no committee reports. A section-by-section analysis of the Act was inserted by Senator Dole, the Senate Minority Leader, into the Congressional Record (S. 15472, October 30, 1991). This analysis was endorsed by thirteen other senators, and was incorporated as the views of the administration by the President in his signing statement. This analysis, however, does not necessarily reflect the views of the majority of the Congress.

The Appendix which follows includes an edited version of the key sections of the Civil Rights Act of 1991. (The largest omission was of the technical provisions relating to employees of the House and Senate.) The "analysis" that follows each statutory section is an excerpt from the section-by-section analysis inserted into the Congressional Record by Senator Dole.

---

# SECTION 1.  SHORT TITLE.

This Act may be cited as the "Civil Rights Act of 1991".

## SEC. 2.  FINDINGS.

The Congress finds that—

(1) additional remedies under Federal law are needed to deter unlawful harassment and intentional discrimination in the workplace;

(2) the decision of the Supreme Court in Wards Cove Packing Co. v. Atonio, 490 U.S. 642 (1989) has weakened the scope and effectiveness of Federal civil rights protections;  and

(3) legislation is necessary to provide additional protections against unlawful discrimination in employment.

## SEC. 3.  PURPOSES.

The purposes of this Act are—

(1) to provide appropriate remedies for intentional discrimination and unlawful harassment in the workplace;

(2) to codify the concepts of "business necessity" and "job related" enunciated by the Supreme Court in Griggs v. Duke Power Co., 401 U.S. 424 (1971), and in the other Supreme Court decisions prior to Wards Cove Packing Co. v. Atonio, 490 U.S. 642 (1989);

(3) to confirm statutory authority and provide statutory guidelines for the adjudication of disparate impact suits under title VII of the Civil Rights Act of 1964 (42 U.S.C. 2000e et seq.); and

(4) to respond to recent decisions of the Supreme Court by expanding the scope of relevant civil rights statutes in order to provide adequate protection to victims of discrimination.

## TITLE I—FEDERAL CIVIL RIGHTS REMEDIES

## SEC. 101. PROHIBITION AGAINST ALL RACIAL DISCRIMINATION IN THE MAKING AND ENFORCEMENT OF CONTRACTS.

Section 1977 of the Revised Statutes (42 U.S.C. 1981) is amended—

(2) by adding at the end the following new subsections:

"(b) For purposes of this section, the term 'make and enforce contracts' includes the making, performance, modification, and termination of contracts, and the enjoyment of all benefits, privileges, terms, and conditions of the contractual relationship.

"(c) The rights protected by this section are protected against impairment by nongovernmental discrimination and impairment under color of State law."

[Legislative Analysis]

*Under 42 U.S.C. 1981, persons of all races have the same right "to make and enforce contracts." In* Patterson v. McLean Credit Union, *109 S.Ct. 2363 (1989), the Supreme Court held: "The most obvious feature of the provision is the restriction of its scope to forbidding discrimination in the 'mak[ing] and enforce[ment]' of contracts alone. Where an alleged act of discrimination does not involve the impairment of one of these specific rights, [sec.] 1981 provides no relief."*

*As written, therefore, section 1981 provides insufficient protection against racial discrimination in the context of contracts. In particular, it provides no relief for discrimination in the performance of contracts (as contrasted with the making and enforcement of contracts). Section 1981, as amended by this Act, will provide a remedy for individuals who are subjected to discriminatory performance of their employment contracts (through racial harassment, for example) or are dismissed or denied promotions because of race. In addition, the discriminatory infringement of contractual rights that do not involve employment will be made actionable under section 1981. This will, for example, create a remedy for a black child who is admitted to a private school as required pursuant to section 1981, but is then subjected to discrimi-*

*natory treatment in the performance of the contract once he or she is attending the school.*

*In addition to overruling the* Patterson *decision, this Section of the Act codifies the holding of* Runyon v. McCrary, *427 U.S. 160 (1976), under which section 1981 prohibits private, as well as governmental, discrimination.*

----

## SEC. 102. DAMAGES IN CASES OF INTENTIONAL DISCRIMINATION.

The Revised Statutes are amended by inserting after section 1977 (42 U.S.C. 1981) the following new section:

## "SEC. 1977A. DAMAGES IN CASES OF INTENTIONAL DISCRIMINATION IN EMPLOYMENT.

"(a) RIGHT OF RECOVERY.

"(1) CIVIL RIGHTS. In an action brought by a complaining party under section 706 or 717 of the Civil Rights Act of 1964 (42 U.S.C. 2000e–5) against a respondent who engaged in unlawful intentional discrimination (not an employment practice that is unlawful because of its disparate impact) prohibited under section 703, 704, or 717 of the Act (42 U.S.C. 2000e–2 or 2000e–3), and provided that the complaining party cannot recover under section 1977 of the Revised Statutes (42 U.S.C. 1981), the complaining party may recover compensatory and punitive damages as allowed in subsection (b), in addition to any relief authorized by section 706(g) of the Civil Rights Act of 1964, from the respondent.

"(2) DISABILITY. In an action brought by a complaining party under the powers, remedies, and procedures set forth in section 706 or 717 of the Civil Rights Act of 1964 (as provided in section 107(a) of the Americans with Disabilities Act of 1990 (42 U.S.C. 12117(a)), and section 505(a)(1) of the Rehabilitation Act of 1973 (29 U.S.C. 794a(a)(1)), respectively) against a respondent who engaged in unlawful intentional discrimination (not an employment practice that is unlawful because of its disparate impact) under section 501 of the Rehabilitation Act of 1973 (29 U.S.C. 791) and the regulations implementing section 501, or who violated the requirements of section 501 of the Act or the regulations implementing section 501 concerning the provision of a reasonable accommodation, or section 102 of the Americans with Disabilities Act of 1990 (42 U.S.C. 12112), or committed a violation of section 102(b)(5) of the Act, against an individual, the complaining party may recover compensatory and punitive damages as allowed in subsection (b), in addition to any relief authorized by section 706(g) of the Civil Rights Act of 1964, from the respondent.

"(3) REASONABLE ACCOMMODATION AND GOOD FAITH EFFORT. In cases where a discriminatory practice involves the provision of a reasonable accommodation pursuant to section 102(b)(5) of the Americans with Disabilities Act of 1990 or regulations implementing section 501 of the Rehabilitation Act of 1973, damages may not be awarded under this section where the covered entity demonstrates good faith efforts, in consultation with the person with the disability who has informed the covered entity that accommodation is needed, to identify and make a reasonable accommodation that would provide such individual with an equally effective opportunity and would not cause an undue hardship on the operation of the business.

"(b) COMPENSATORY AND PUNITIVE DAMAGES.

"(1) DETERMINATION OF PUNITIVE DAMAGES. A complaining party may recover punitive damages under this section against a respondent (other than a government, government agency or political subdivision) if the complaining party demonstrates that the respondent engaged in a discriminatory practice or discriminatory practices with malice or with reckless indifference to the federally protected rights of an aggrieved individual.

"(2) EXCLUSIONS FROM COMPENSATORY DAMAGES. Compensatory damages awarded under this section shall not include backpay, interest on backpay, or any other type of relief authorized under section 706(g) of the Civil Rights Act of 1964.

"(3) LIMITATIONS. The sum of the amount of compensatory damages awarded under this section for future pecuniary losses, emotional pain, suffering, inconvenience, mental anguish, loss of enjoyment of life, and other nonpecuniary losses, and the amount of punitive damages awarded under this section, shall not exceed, for each complaining party—

"(A) in the case of a respondent who has more than 14 and fewer than 101 employees in each of 20 or more calendar weeks in the current or preceding calendar year, $50,000;

"(B) in the case of a respondent who has more than 100 and fewer than 201 employees in each of 20 or more calendar weeks in the current or preceding calendar year, $100,000; and

"(C) in the case of a respondent who has more than 200 and fewer than 501 employees in each of 20 or more calendar weeks in the current or preceding calendar year, $200,000; and

"(D) in the case of a respondent who has more than 500 employees in each of 20 or more calendar weeks in the current or preceding calendar year, $300,000.

"(4) CONSTRUCTION. Nothing in this section shall be construed to limit the scope of, or the relief available under, section 1977 of the Revised Statutes (42 U.S.C. 1981)."

———

[Legislative Analysis]

*[This] section makes available compensatory and punitive damages in cases involving intentional discrimination brought under Title VII of the Civil Rights Act of 1964 and the Americans with Disabilities Act. It sets an important precedent in tort reform by setting caps on those damages, including pecuniary losses that have not yet occurred as of the time the charge is filed, as well as all emotional pain, suffering, inconvenience, mental anguish, loss of enjoyment of life, and other nonpecuniary losses, whenever they occur. Punitive damages are also capped, and are to be awarded only in extraordinarily egregious cases. The damages contemplated in this section are to be available in cases challenging unlawful affirmative action plans, quotas, and other preferences.*

———

"(c) JURY TRIAL. If a complaining party seeks compensatory or punitive damages under this section—

"(1) any party may demand a trial by jury; and

"(2) the court shall not inform the jury of the limitations described in subsection (b)(3)."

## SEC. 104. DEFINITIONS.

Section 701 of the Civil Rights Act of 1964 (42 U.S.C. 2000e) is amended by adding at the end the following new subsections:

"(1) The term 'complaining party' means the Commission, the Attorney General, or a person who may bring an action or proceeding under this title.

"(m) The term 'demonstrates' means meets the burdens of production and persuasion.

"(n) The term 'respondent' means an employer, employment agency, labor organization, joint labor-management committee controlling apprenticeship or other training or retraining program, including an on-the-job training program, or Federal entity subject to section 717.".

## SEC. 105. BURDEN OF PROOF IN DISPARATE IMPACT CASES.

(a) Section 703 of the Civil Rights Act of 1964 (42 U.S.C. 2000e–2) is amended by adding at the end the following new subsection:

"(k)(1)(A) An unlawful employment practice based on disparate impact is established under this title only if—

"(i) a complaining party demonstrates that a respondent uses a particular employment practice that causes a disparate impact on the basis of race, color, religion, sex, or national origin and the respondent fails to demonstrate that the challenged practice is job related for the position in question and consistent with business necessity; or

"(ii) the complaining party makes the demonstration described in subparagraph (C) with respect to an alternative employment practice and the respondent refuses to adopt such alternative employment practice.

"(B)(i) With respect to demonstrating that a particular employment practice causes a disparate impact as described in subparagraph (A)(i), the complaining party shall demonstrate that each particular challenged employment practice causes a disparate impact, except that if the complaining party can demonstrate to the court that the elements of a respondent's decisionmaking process are not capable of separation for analysis, the decisionmaking process may be analyzed as one employment practice.

"(ii) If the respondent demonstrates that a specific employment practice does not cause the disparate impact, the respondent shall not be required to demonstrate that such practice is required by business necessity.

"(C) The demonstration referred to by subparagraph (A)(ii) shall be in accordance with the law as it existed on June 4, 1989, with respect to the concept of 'alternative employment practice'.

"(2) A demonstration that an employment practice is required by business necessity may not be used as a defense against a claim of intentional discrimination under this title.

"(3) Notwithstanding any other provision of this title, a rule barring the employment of an individual who currently and knowingly uses or possesses a controlled substance, as defined in schedules I and II of section 102(6) of the Controlled Substances Act (21 U.S.C. 802(6)), other than the use or possession of a drug taken under the supervision of a licensed health care professional, or any other use or possession authorized by the Controlled Substances Act or any other provision of Federal law, shall be considered an unlawful employment practice under this title only if such rule is adopted or applied with an intent to discriminate because of race, color, religion, sex, or national origin.".

---

[Legislative Analysis]

\* \* \*

*Under this Act, a complaining party makes out a prima facie case of disparate impact when he or she identifies a particular selection practice and demonstrates that the practice has caused a disparate impact on the basis of race, color, religion, sex, or national origin. The burden of proof then shifts to the respondent to demonstrate that the practice is justified by business necessity. It is then open to the complaining party to rebut that defense by demonstrating the availability of an alternative selection practice, comparable in cost and equally effective in measuring job performance or achieving the respondent's legitimate employment goals, that will reduce the disparate impact, and that the respondent refuses to adopt such alternative.*

*The burden-of-proof issue that* Wards Cove *resolved in favor of defendants is resolved by this Act in favor of plaintiffs.* Wards Cove *is thereby overruled. As the narrow title of the Section and its plain language show, however, on all other issues this Act leaves existing law undisturbed.*

### The requirement of particularity

*The bill leaves unchanged the longstanding requirement that a plaintiff identify the particular practice which he or she is challenging in a disparate impact case.*

\* \* \*

### The defendant's evidentiary standard: Job relatedness and business necessity

*The bill embodies longstanding concepts of job-relatedness and business necessity and rejects proposed innovations. In short, it repre-*

*sents an affirmation of existing law, including* Wards Cove.

————

## SEC. 106. PROHIBITION AGAINST DISCRIMINATORY USE OF TEST SCORES.

Section 703 of the Civil Rights Act of 1964 (42 U.S.C. 2000e–2) (as amended by section 105) is further amended by adding at the end the following new subsection:

"(1) It shall be an unlawful employment practice for a respondent, in connection with the selection or referral of applicants or candidates for employment or promotion, to adjust the scores of, use different cutoff scores for, or otherwise alter the results of, employment related tests on the basis of race, color, religion, sex, or national origin.".

————

[Legislative Analysis]

*Section [106] means exactly what it says: race-norming or any other discriminatory adjustment of scores or cutoff points of any employment related test is illegal. This means, for instance, that discriminatory use of the Generalized Aptitude Test Battery (GATB) by the Department of Labor and state employment agencies is illegal. It also means that race-norming may not be ordered by a court as part of the remedy in any case, nor may it be approved by a court as a part of a consent decree, when done because of the disparate impact of those test scores. See* Bridgeport Guardians, Inc. v. City of Bridgeport, *933 F.2d 1140 (2d Cir.1991).*

*It is important to note, too, that this section in no way be interpreted to discourage employers from using tests. Frequently tests are good predictors and helpful tools for employers to use. Indeed, Title VII contains a provision specifically designed to protect the use of tests. See 42 U.S.C. 2000e–2(h). Rather, the section intends only to ban the discriminatory adjustment of test scores or cutoffs.*

———

SEC. 107. CLARIFYING PROHIBITION AGAINST IMPERMISSIBLE CONSIDERATION OF RACE, COLOR, RELIGION, SEX, OR NATIONAL ORIGIN IN EMPLOYMENT PRACTICES.

(a) IN GENERAL. Section 703 of the Civil Rights Act of 1964 (42 U.S.C. 2000e–2) (as amended by sections 105 and 106) is further amended by adding at the end the following new subsection:

"(m) Except as otherwise provided in this title, an unlawful employment practice is established when the complaining party demonstrates that race, color, religion, sex, or national origin was a motivating factor for any employment practice, even though other factors also motivated the practice.".

(b) ENFORCEMENT PROVISIONS. Section 706(g) of such Act (42 U.S.C. 2000e–5(g)) is amended—

\* \* \*

(3) by adding at the end the following new subparagraph:

"(B) On a claim in which an individual proves a violation under section 703(m) and a respondent demonstrates that the respondent would have taken the same action in the absence of the impermissible motivating factor, the court—

"(i) may grant declaratory relief, injunctive relief (except as provided in clause (ii)), and attorney's fees and costs demonstrated to be directly attributable only to the pursuit of a claim under section 703(m); and

"(ii) shall not award damages or issue an order requiring any admission, reinstatement, hiring, promotion, or payment, described in subparagraph (A).".

---

[Legislative Analysis]

*[This] section of the bill addresses the holding in* Price Waterhouse v. Hopkins, *109*

*S.Ct. 1775 (1989), in which the Court ruled in favor of the woman who alleged that she had been denied partnership by her accounting firm on account of her sex. The Court there faced a case in which the plaintiff alleged that her gender had supplied part of the motivation of her rejection for partnership. The Court held that once she had established by direct evidence that sex played a substantial part in the decision, the employer could still defeat liability by showing that it would have reached the same decision had sex not been considered.*

*Section 10 allows the employer to be held liable if discrimination was a motivating factor in causing the harm suffered by the complainant. Thus, such discrimination need not have been the sole cause of the final decision.*

*The provision also makes clear that if an employer establishes that it would have taken the same employment action absent consideration of race, sex, color, religion, or national origin, the complainant is not entitled to reinstatement, backpay, or damages.*

*It should also be stressed that this provision is equally applicable to cases involving challenges to unlawful affirmative action plans, quotas, and other preferences.*

## SEC. 108. FACILITATING PROMPT AND ORDERLY RESOLUTION OF CHALLENGES TO EMPLOYMENT PRACTICES IMPLEMENTING LITIGATED OR CONSENT JUDGMENTS OR ORDERS.

Section 703 of the Civil Rights Act of 1964 (42 U.S.C. 2000e–2) (as amended by sections 105, 106, and 107 of this title) is further amended by adding at the end the following new subsection:

"(n)(1)(A) Notwithstanding any other provision of law, and except as provided in paragraph (2), an employment practice that implements and is within the scope of a litigated or consent judgment or order that resolves a claim of employment discrimination under the Constitution or Federal civil rights laws may not be challenged under the circumstances described in subparagraph (B).

"(B) A practice described in subparagraph (A) may not be challenged in a claim under the Constitution or Federal civil rights laws—

"(i) by a person who, prior to the entry of the judgment or order described in subparagraph (A), had—

"(I) actual notice of the proposed judgment or order sufficient to apprise such person that such judgment or order might adversely affect the interests and legal rights of such person and that an opportunity was

available to present objections to such judgment or order by a future date certain; and

"(II) a reasonable opportunity to present
objections to such judgment or order; or

"(ii) by a person whose interests were
adequately represented by another person
who had previously challenged the judgment
or order on the same legal grounds and with
a similar factual situation, unless there has
been an intervening change in law or fact."

\* \* \*

---

[Legislative Analysis]

*In* Hansberry v. Lee, *311 U.S. 32, 40–41
(1940) the Supreme Court held:*

*"It is a principle of general application in
Anglo–American jurisprudence that one is
not bound by a judgment in personam in
which he is not designated as a party or to
which he has not been made a party by
service of process.  \* \* \* A judgment rendered in such circumstances is not entitled to
the full faith and credit which the Constitution and statutes of the United States \* \* \*
prescribe, \* \* \* and judicial action enforcing
it against the person or property of the absent
party is not that due process which the Fifth
and Fourteenth Amendments require."*

*In* Hansberry, *Carl Hansberry and his family, who were black, were seeking to challenge a racial covenant prohibiting the sale of land to blacks. One of the owners who wanted the covenant enforced argued that the Hansberrys could not litigate the validity of the convenant because that question has previously been adjudicated, and the covenant sustained, in an earlier lawsuit, although the Hansberrys were not parties in that lawsuit. The Illinois court had ruled that the Hansberrys' challenge was barred, but the Supreme court found that this ruling violated due process and allowed the challenge.*

*In* Martin v. Wilks, *109 S.Ct. 2180 (1989), the Court confronted a similar argument. That case involved a claim by Robert Wilks and other white fire fighters that the City of Birmingham had discriminated against them by refusing to promote them because of their race. The City argued that their challenge was barred because the City's promotion process had been sanctioned in a consent decree entered in an earlier case between the City and a class of black plaintiffs, of which Wilks and the white fire fighters were aware, but in which they were not parties. The Court rejected this argument. Instead, it concluded that the Federal Rules of Civil Procedure required that persons seeking to bind outsiders to the results of litigation have a duty to join them as parties, see Fed.R.Civ.P. 19, unless the court certified a class of defendants adequately represented by a named defendant, see Fed.R.Civ.P. 23. The Court specifically rejected the defendants' argument that a different rule should obtain in civil rights litigation.*

*Under specified conditions, Section 11 of the bill would preclude certain challenges to employment practices specifically required by court orders or judgments entered in Title VII cases. This Section would bar such challenges by any person who was an employee, former employee, or applicant for employment during the notice period and who, prior to the entry of the judgment or order, received notice of the judgment in sufficient detail to apprise that person that the judgment or order would likely affect that person's interests and legal rights; of the relief in the proposed judgment; that a reasonable opportunity was available to that person to challenge the judgment or order by future date certain; and that the person would likely be barred from challenging the proposed judgment after that date. The intent of this section is to protect valid decrees from subsequent attack by individuals who were fully apprised of their interest in litigation and given an opportunity to participate, but who declined that opportunity.*

*In particular, the phrase "actual notice
\* \* \* appris[ing] such person that such judgment or order might adversely affect the interests and legal rights of such person,"
means of course that the notice itself must
make clear that potential adverse effect.
And this, in turn, means also that the discriminatory practice at issue must be clearly
a part of the judgment or order. Otherwise,
it cannot credibly be asserted that the potential plaintiff was given adequate notice.
Thus, where it is only by later judicial gloss
or by the earlier parties' implementation of
the judgment or order that the allegedly discriminatory practice becomes clear, Section
11 would not bar a subsequent challenge.
Moreover, the adverse effect on the person
barred must be a likely or probable one, not a
mere possibility. Otherwise, people would be
encouraged to rush into court to defend
against any remote risk to their rights, thus
unnecessarily complicating litigation. Finally, the notice must include notice of the fact
that the person must assert his or her rights
or lose them. Otherwise, it will be insufficient to apprise the individual "that such
judgment or order might adversely affect"
his or her interests.*

*"Adequate representation" requires that the
person enjoy a privity of interest with the later
party. This is because in Section 11 both
"(n)(1)(B)(i)" and "(n)(1)(B)(ii)" must be construed*

with *"(n)(2)(D)"* so that people's due process rights are not jeopardized. And the Supreme Court has stated clearly: *"It is a violation of due process for a judgment to be binding on a litigant who was not a party or a privy and therefore never had an opportunity to be heard."* Parklane Hosiery Co. v. Shore, *439 U.S. 322, 327 n. 7 (1979).*

———

## SEC. 109. PROTECTION OF EXTRATERRITORIAL EMPLOYMENT.

(a) DEFINITION OF EMPLOYEE. Section 701(f) of the Civil Rights Act of 1964 (42 U.S.C. 2000e(f)) and section 101(4) of the Americans with Disabilities Act of 1990 (42 U.S.C. 12111(4)) are each amended by adding at the end the following: "With respect to employment in a foreign country, such term includes an individual who is a citizen of the United States.".

\* \* \*

———

[Legislative Analysis]

*Section [109] extends the protections of Title VII and the ADA extraterritorially. It adopts the same language as the ADEA to achieve this end.*

*In addition, the section makes clear that employers are not required to take actions otherwise prohibited by law in a foreign place of business.*

———

## SEC. 112. EXPANSION OF RIGHT TO CHALLENGE DISCRIMINATORY SENIORITY SYSTEMS.

Section 706(e) of the Civil Rights Act of 1964 (42 U.S.C. 2000e–5(e)) is amended—

\* \* \*

(2) by adding at the end the following new paragraph:

"(2) For purposes of this section, an unlawful employment practice occurs, with respect to a seniority system that has been adopted for an intentionally discriminatory purpose in violation of this title (whether or not that discriminatory purpose is apparent on the face of the seniority provision), when the seniority system is adopted, when an individual becomes subject to the seniority system, or when a person aggrieved is injured by the application of the seniority system or provision of the system.".

———

### [Legislative Analysis]

*Section [112] overrules the holding in* Lorance v. AT & T Technologies, Inc., *109 S.Ct. 2261 (1989), in which female employees challenged a seniority sys-*

*tem pursuant to Title VII, claiming that it was adopted with an intent to discriminate against women. Although the system was facially nondiscriminatory and treated all similarly situated employees alike, it produced demotions for the plaintiffs, who claimed that the employer had adopted the seniority system with the intention of altering their contractual rights. The Supreme Court held that the claim was barred by Title VII's requirement that a charge must be filed within 180 days (or 300 days if the matter can be referred to a state agency) after the alleged discrimination occurred.*

\* \* \*

*Section 14 is not intended to disturb the settled law that disparate impact challenges may not be brought against seniority systems. See* TWA v. Hardison, *432 U.S. 63, 82 (1977);* American Tobacco Co. v. Patterson, *456 U.S. 63, 65, 69 (1982);* Pullman–Standard v. Swint, *456 U.S. 273, 289 (1982).*

———

SEC. 113. AUTHORIZING AWARD OF EXPERT FEES.

(a) REVISED STATUTES. Section 722 of the Revised Statutes is amended—

\* \* \*

(2) by adding at the end the following new subsection:

Player, Empl.Discrim.NS 3rd—12

"(c) In awarding an attorney's fee under subsection (b) in any action or proceeding to enforce a provision of sections 1977 or 1977A of the Revised Statutes, the court, in its discretion, may include expert fees as part of the attorney's fee.".

(b) CIVIL RIGHTS ACT OF 1964. Section 706(k) of the Civil Rights Act of 1964 (42 U.S.C. 2000e–5(k)) is amended by inserting "(including expert fees)" after "attorney's fee".

---

### [Legislative Analysis]

*Section [113] authorizes the recovery of a reasonable expert witness fee by prevailing parties. See* West Virginia University Hospitals, Inc. v. Casey, *No. 89–994 (U.S.Sup.Ct. Mar. 19, 1991); cf.* Crawford Fitting Co. v. J.T. Gibbons, Inc., *482 U.S. 437 (1987). The provision is intended to allow recovery for work done in preparation of trial as well as after trial has begun.*

*In exercising its discretion, the court should ensure that fees are kept within reasonable bounds. Fees should never exceed the amount actually paid to the expert, or the going rate for such work, whichever is lower.*

---

## SEC. 114. PROVIDING FOR INTEREST AND EXTENDING THE STATUTE OF LIMITATIONS IN ACTIONS AGAINST THE FEDERAL GOVERNMENT.

Section 717 of the Civil Rights Act of 1964 (42 U.S.C. 2000e–16) is amended—

(1) in subsection (c), by striking "thirty days" and inserting "90 days"; and

(2) in subsection (d), by inserting before the period ", and the same interest to compensate for delay in payment shall be available as in cases involving nonpublic parties.".

———

### [Legislative Analysis]

*Section [114] extends the period for filing a complaint against the Federal government pursuant to Title VII from 30 days to 90 days. It also authorizes the payment of interest to compensate for delay in the payment of a judgment according to the same rules that govern such payments in actions against private parties.*

———

## SEC. 115. NOTICE OF LIMITATIONS PERIOD UNDER THE AGE DISCRIMINATION IN EMPLOYMENT ACT OF 1967.

Section 7(e) of the Age Discrimination in Employment Act of 1967 (29 U.S.C. 626(e)) is amended—

(1) by striking paragraph (2);

(2) by striking the paragraph designation in paragraph (1);

(3) by striking "Sections 6 and" and inserting "Section"; and

(4) by adding at the end the following:

"If a charge filed with the Commission under this Act is dismissed or the proceedings of the Commission are otherwise terminated by the Commission, the Commission shall notify the person aggrieved. A civil action may be brought under this section by a person defined in section 11(a) against the respondent named in the charge within 90 days after the date of the receipt of such notice.".

————

### [Legislative Analysis]

*This section generally conforms procedures for filing charges under the ADEA with those used for other portions of Title VII. In particular, it provides that the EEOC shall notify individuals who have filed charges of the dismissal or completion of the Commis-*

*sion's proceedings with respect to those charges, and allows those individuals to file suit from 60 days after filing the charge until the expiration of 90 days after completion of those proceedings. This avoids the problems created by current law, which imposes a statute of limitations on the filing of suit regardless of whether the EEOC has completed its action on an individual's charge.*

————

## SEC. 117. COVERAGE OF HOUSE OF REPRESENTATIVES AND THE AGENCIES OF THE LEGISLATIVE BRANCH.

(a) COVERAGE OF THE HOUSE OF REPRESENTATIVES.—

(1) IN GENERAL. Notwithstanding any provision of title VII of the Civil Rights Act of 1964 (42 U.S.C. 2000e et seq.) or of other law, the purposes of such title shall, subject to paragraph (2), apply in their entirety to the House of Representatives.

\* \* \*

## SEC. 302. DISCRIMINATORY PRACTICES PROHIBITED.

All personnel actions affecting employees of the Senate shall be made free from any discrimination based on—

(1) race, color, religion, sex, or national origin, within the meaning of section 717 of the Civil Rights Act of 1964 (42 U.S.C. 2000e–16);

(2) age, within the meaning of section 15 of the Age Discrimination in Employment Act of 1967 (29 U.S.C. 633a); or

(3) handicap or disability, within the meaning of section 501 of the Rehabilitation Act of 1973 (29 U.S.C. 791) and sections 102–104 of the Americans with Disabilities Act of 1990 (42 U.S.C. 12112–14).

\* \* \*

---

### [Author's Note]

*The above sections provide statutory protection to congressional employees. Enforcement is initially through internal procedures. Senate employees or members of the Senate aggrieved by the final internal order may secure limited review in the U.S. Court of Appeals for the Federal Circuit.*

## SEC. 320. COVERAGE OF PRESIDENTIAL APPOINTEES.

(a) IN GENERAL.—

(1) APPLICATION. The rights, protections, and remedies provided pursuant to section 302 of this title shall apply with respect to employment of Presidential appointees.

\* \* \*

(b) PRESIDENTIAL APPOINTEE. For purposes of this section, the term "Presidential appointee" means any officer or employee, or an applicant seeking to become an officer or employee, in any unit of the Executive Branch, including the Executive Office of the President, whether appointed by the President or by any other appointing authority in the Executive Branch, who is not already entitled to bring an action under any of the statutes referred to in section 302 but does not include any individual—

> (1) whose appointment is made by and with the advice and consent of the Senate;

> (2) who is appointed to an advisory committee, as defined in section 3(2) of the Federal Advisory Committee Act (5 U.S.C.App.); or

> (3) who is a member of the uniformed services.

\* \* \*

## SEC. 321. COVERAGE OF PREVIOUSLY EXEMPT STATE EMPLOYEES.

(a) APPLICATION. The rights, protections, and remedies provided pursuant to section 302 of this title shall apply with respect to employment of any individual chosen or appointed, by a person elected to public office in any State or political subdivision of any State by the qualified voters thereof—

(1) to be a member of the elected official's personal staff;

(2) to serve the elected official on the policy-making level; or

(3) to serve the elected official as an immediate advisor with respect to the exercise of the constitutional or legal powers of the office.

---

### [Authors Note]

*Section 320 extends protection to Presidential appointees (a result of the Thomas confirmation?). Section 321 removes the implicit exclusion of employment decisions affecting high policy makers of state and local government officials. Sections 320 and 321 are enforced similarly, but differently from any other provisions of Title VII. An aggrieved individual must file a charge with the EEOC within 180 days of the discriminatory act. The EEOC shall hear and and make a final determination of whether a violation of the Act has occurred. The EEOC findings will be subject to limited judicial review under 28 U.S.C.A. Chapter 158. Such review allows the court to set aside findings of the EEOC if they are: (1) arbitrary, capricious, an abuse of discretion, or not consistent with the law; (2) not made consistent with required procedures; or (3) unsupported by substantial evidence on the record created in the EEOC proceeding.*

## SEC. 402.   EFFECTIVE DATE.

(a) IN GENERAL.   Except as otherwise specifically provided, this Act and the amendments made by this Act shall take effect upon enactment.

### [Legislative Analysis]

*  *  * [T]he Act and the amendments made by the Act take effect upon enactment. Accordingly, they will not apply to cases arising before the effective date of the Act. At the request of the Senators from Alaska, section 22(b) specifically points out that nothing in the Act will apply retroactively to the Wards Cove Packing Company, an Alaska company that spent 24 years defending against a disparate impact challenge.*

\*

# INDEX

---

References are to Pages

---

315

†